Ethical Economy. Studies in Economic Ethics and Philosophy

Volume 54

Ethical Economy describes the theory of the ethical preconditions of the economy and of business as well as the theory of the ethical foundations of economic systems. It analyzes the impact of rules, virtues, and goods or values on economic action and management. *Ethical Economy* understands ethics as a means to increase trust and to reduce transaction costs. It forms a foundational theory for business ethics and business culture.

The Series *Ethical Economy. Studies in Economic Ethics and Philosophy* is devoted to the investigation of interdisciplinary issues concerning economics, management, ethics, and philosophy. These issues fall in the categories of economic ethics, business ethics, management theory, economic culture, and economic philosophy, the latter including the epistemology and ontology of economics. Economic culture comprises cultural and hermeneutic studies of the economy.

One goal of the series is to extend the discussion of the philosophical, ethical, and cultural foundations of economics and economic systems. The series is intended to serve as an international forum for scholarly publications, such as monographs, conference proceedings, and collections of essays. Primary emphasis is placed on originality, clarity, and interdisciplinary synthesis of elements from economics, management theory, ethics, and philosophy.

More information about this series at http://www.springer.com/series/2881

Jakob Bek-Thomsen • Christian Olaf Christiansen
Stefan Gaarsmand Jacobsen • Mikkel Thorup
Editors

History of Economic Rationalities

Economic Reasoning as Knowledge and Practice Authority

This book and the research of its editors was first and foremost made possible through the generous funding of Velux Fonden. Furthermore, The Danish Council for Independent Research supported the editing of the book in its final stages.

Springer

Editors
Jakob Bek-Thomsen
Institute for Culture and Society
Aarhus University
Aarhus, Denmark

Christian Olaf Christiansen
Institute for Culture and Society
Aarhus University
Aarhus, Denmark

Stefan Gaarsmand Jacobsen
Department of Management, Politics and Philosophy
Copenhagen Business School
Frederiksberg, Denmark

Mikkel Thorup
Institute for Culture and Society
Aarhus University
Aarhus, Denmark

ISSN 2211-2707 ISSN 2211-2723 (electronic)
Ethical Economy
ISBN 978-3-319-52814-4 ISBN 978-3-319-52815-1 (eBook)
DOI 10.1007/978-3-319-52815-1

Library of Congress Control Number: 2017934076

Printed on acid-free paper

This Springer imprint is published by Springer Nature
The registered company is Springer International Publishing AG
The registered company address is: Gewerbestrasse 11, 6330 Cham, Switzerland

Contents

About the Authors

Jakob Bek-Thomsen is assistant professor at Aarhus University, Institute for Culture and Society. He has worked with both the history of medicine and economic thinking during the Renaissance with a particular attention as to how humanist movements and ideas influenced and informed other areas of knowledge. His current research is connected with modern medicine and its understanding of death in connection with terminal illness.

Mark Bevir is a professor in the Department of Political Science, University of California, Berkeley. He is the author or co-author of *The Logic of the History of Ideas* (1999), *Interpreting British Governance* (2003), *New Labour: A Critique* (2005), *Governance Stories* (2006), *Key Concepts of Governance* (2009), *The State as Cultural Practice* (2010), *Democratic Governance* (2010), *The Making of British Socialism* (2011), *Governance: A Very Short Introduction* (2012) and *A Theory of Governance* (2013).

Jill Marie Bradbury is a professor in the Department of English at Gallaudet University. She became interested in the history of economic thought while double majoring in economics and English as an undergraduate. Since receiving her PhD at Brown University, she has published several essays on eighteenth-century economic discourse, including 'Interest and Anglo-Irish Political Discourses in the 1720–1721 Bank Pamphlet Literature' in *Eighteenth-Century Ireland* and 'Domestic, Moral, and Political Economies in Swift's Irish Writings' in *Anglo-Irish Identities*, 1571–1845, which she also coedited. She is currently working on a book titled *British Economic Discourses, 1650–1750*, and her master's degree in economics at George Mason University.

Christian Olaf Christiansen is associate professor at Aarhus University, Institute for Culture and Society. Christian is an intellectual historian working with twentieth-century economic and political thought in an American and global context. His current research is a comparative intellectual history of two approaches to inequality and poverty reduction during post-war globalisation: socio-economic human rights and market–/business-based ideas for poverty reduction. Earlier publications include *Progressive Business: An Intellectual History of the Role of Business in Society* (with Oxford University Press, 2015).

Erwin Dekker is assistant professor in cultural economics at the Erasmus University in Rotterdam and postdoctoral fellow at the George Mason University Department of Economics. He has recently published *The Viennese Students of Civilization* with Cambridge University Press. His research focuses on every area where art and culture meet economics. He has published in the fields of cultural economics, economic methodology and intellectual history, and he is currently working on exemplary goods and moral frameworks.

Christoffer Basse Eriksen is a doctoral student at the Department of Philosophy and History of Ideas at Aarhus University. His interests lie in the interrelationship between early modern natural philosophy and the history of the life sciences. In his dissertation, he examines the early uses of the microscope in the seventeenth century and especially the emergence of the microorganic realm of nature. He has written reviews for the *Journal of Early Modern Studies*, *Preternature*, *Intellectual History Review* and *Early Science and Medicine*.

Stefan Gaarsmand Jacobsen is a postdoctoral researcher at Copenhagen Business School, working on the historical trajectories of radical economic thought. His current project is about the struggles inside the climate movement to create a powerful response to the corporate dominance of political economy since the late 1990s. He is currently editing the anthology *Climate Justice and the Economy* with Routledge. His previous research has been published in *Journal of Early Modern History*, *Journal of World History* and *Journal for Eighteenth-Century Studies*.

Thomas Palmelund Johansen is a PhD candidate in the history of ideas at the Department of Culture and Society, Aarhus University. He has taught modules on history of science, scientific method and theories of professions and is currently working towards the completion of a dissertation on the role of economic ideas in the debates on print, popular education and 'useful knowledge' in late-Georgian England. His work has been published in Scandinavian and international journals and volumes.

Campbell Jones is Associate Professor of Sociology at the University of Auckland, where he teaches finance, critical theory and the sociology and politics of work. He is also a Researcher at the think tank Economic and Social Research Aotearoa, where he conducts collaborative research on work, political organisation and economic planning. He is author of numerous books and articles and is currently writing a book on the nature of work.

Katherine E. Kenny is a postdoctoral research fellow in sociology in the School of Social Sciences at the University of New South Wales, Sydney Australia. She combines disciplinary training in sociology and science and technology studies with research interests in health and illness, biopolitics, neoliberalism, globalisation and the politics of knowledge production. She is currently working on a project investigating the social meanings of cancer survivorship for patients, their careers and health professionals.

Catherine Secretan is senior researcher at the Centre National de la Recherche Scientifique (France). She has published many scholarly papers, monographs and translations on Dutch political ideas in the Early Modern Period (sixteenth to seventeenth century). Among her recent work is 'Lambert van Velthuysen. A Letter on the Principles of Justness and Decency: Containing a Defence of the Treatise De Cive of the Learned Mr. Hobbes', with Malcolm de Mowbray (2013); *In praise of Ordinary People: Early Modern Britain and the Dutch Republic*, with Margaret C. Jacob (2013); and *Les Pays-Bas aux XVIIe et XVIIIe Siècles: Nouveaux Regards*, with Delphine Antoine-Mahut (2015).

Mikkel Thorup is professor with special responsibilities in market cultures and the history of political thought at the Institute of Culture and Society, University of Aarhus, Denmark. Thorup is the author and editor of numerous books, including *An Intellectual History of Terror* (2010), *Rousseau and Revolution* (with Holger Lauritsen, 2010), *Intellectual History: 5 Questions* (with Morten H Jeppesen and Frederik Stjernfelt, 2013), *Pro Bono* (2015), *The Total Enemy* (2015) and *Intellectual History of Economic Normativities* (2016). Thorup was the principal investigator on the research project ECORA behind this publication.

Niccolò Valmori obtained an MA in history from the University of Milan working on the first period of the French revolution. At the European University Institute, he defended a PhD thesis by the title 'Private interest and public sphere: finance and politics in France, England and the Netherlands during the Age of Revolution, 1789–1810'. His main fields of interest are French revolution, Atlantic history and economic history.

Laurens van Apeldoorn is assistant professor in philosophy at Leiden University, the Netherlands. His research interests include early modern political thought, in particular the philosophy of Thomas Hobbes, and contemporary political theory. He obtained a DPhil degree in political theory at the University of Oxford and has held visiting positions at the University of Montreal and University of Toronto.

Chapter 1
Introduction

Jakob Bek-Thomsen, Christian Olaf Christiansen, Stefan Gaarsmand Jacobsen, and Mikkel Thorup

Economics has become extremely influential as a way we think about the world. Economic science and its highly sophisticated use of mathematics and statistics has become an experts' discourse: one which provides a crucial context for governing our societies, while remaining ever more incomprehensible and esoteric for many of us. Whether speaking of the government of the state, the corporation, the public sector, or of the self, economic reasoning today is a crucial mode of thinking.

As French legal scholar Alain Supiot (2012, 58) notes, we are increasingly living in a world where "government by laws gives way to government by numbers," which "aims at producing a self-regulating human society." This governance by numbers, Supiot explains, "relies on *calculation* – that is, on acts of *quantification* (subsuming different beings and situations under the same unit of account) and on *programming* behaviour (through techniques of benchmarking and ranking)." But economic rationality not only has to do with the role of numbers, quantifications, money and profits as universal principles of equivalence. In its most extreme form, as in the Chicago School economics of Gary Becker, or in the economics imperialism of the Freakonomics crowd and others, all forms of behaviour can be studied as applied "economic rationality."

This is a book about economic rationality. More precisely, it is a book about economic rationalit*ies*, as we argue that there is not one economic rationality but many. Moreover, ours is a *historical* approach: we believe that economic rationalities – in whatever form they may take – are profoundly historically contingent and dependent. We also believe that history helps shed light on the present, and on how

J. Bek-Thomsen (✉) • C.O. Christiansen • M. Thorup
Institute for Culture and Society, Aarhus University, Aarhus, Denmark
e-mail: idejbt@cas.au.dk; idecoc@cas.au.dk; idemt@cas.au.dk

S.G. Jacobsen
Department of Management, Politics and Philosophy, Copenhagen Business School, Frederiksberg, Denmark
e-mail: sgj.mpp@cbs.dk

J. Bek-Thomsen et al. (eds.), *History of Economic Rationalities*, Ethical Economy 54, DOI 10.1007/978-3-319-52815-1_1

specific modes of economic reasoning and calculating became immensely powerful forms of discourse. History, as already Hegel reminded us, provides us with opportunities of understanding how we came to be in a particular way. Marx added that material conditions were more important than ideational ones. Today, we stand at a point where ideas as well as their material and economic contexts are given more equal priority, which many chapters in this book illustrate. And at a time in which many academic fields are becoming more and more specialized, we believe that one of the very merits of intellectual history is its ability to tell stories that tries to capture a kind of wholeness of historical development.

Through multiple case-studies, situated in different historical contexts of the modern West, we aim to show that the development of economic rationalities takes place in the meeting with other regimes of thought, values, and discourses. Regimes of thought and legitimizations of action draw upon systematized authorities of religious, juridical, moral, scientific and increasingly economic reasoning. These authoritative languages interrelate in various ways. They compete to be the prime, societal authority; they supplant each other; they borrow metaphors, concepts, practices; they subvert and change existing languages. Economic rationalities have never existed in isolation but always in conversation and in conflict with other forms of reasoning.

As an analytical concept, economic rationality can refer to at least three things. First, it can refer to *particular kinds of economic reasoning* which draw upon, for example, neoclassical economics. As such, economic reasoning is a particular way of thinking about allocation, distribution, making of prices, efficiency, equilibrium, utility. Second, it can refer to the *role of economic arguments in public debates*, as opposed to other forms of arguments, where, for example, the construction of a highway is deemed economically but not environmentally sound, or where one's investment in a particular education will yield a better pay-off than another one. Third, it can refer to the *legitimacy* of various kinds of economic actions and practices. In this book, all three of these aspects are touched upon in the different chapters – and often overlapping with one another.

***

This book offers fresh and novel insights into the history of economic rationalities. It thereby follows a recent trend towards an "economic turn" in the humanities. More specifically, the cultural (Ray and Sayer 1999; Throsby 2001; du Gay and Pryke 2002) as well as metaphorical and rhetorical (Shell 1982; McCloskey 1985, 1990, 1994; Henderson et al. 1993; Mirowski 1994; Klamer 2007) properties of economics and the economy are now a major field as are increasingly its moral properties. The mid-twentieth century economist John Kenneth Galbraith once wrote that "man cannot live without economic theology – without some rationalizations of the abstract and seemingly inchoate arrangements which provide him with his livelihood" (Galbraith 1956, 17). Galbraith may have captured the very essence of what intellectual histories of economic rationalities is about, in the above sense which focuses upon *legitimacy*: Studying how historical actors have justified and legitimized their economic practices (Skinner 2002). Through a sometimes creative appropriation of historically specific values and discursive patterns, individuals and groups in society have sought to procure moral legitimacy for actions hitherto considered amoral or just not relevant as economic practices. Today, most histories of the moral dimension of economy would probably refrain from asking questions about what came first – a change of discourse and moral evaluation or economic change. What still needs further study is, rather, the intersection of moral discourse and economic activity as it evolves and changes through history.

While this book several times touches upon the history of economic thought, it is thus important to stress that this book is not a contribution to the history of economic science *per se*. It is rather a contribution to an understanding of the histories of economic rationalities *outside* the economics discipline proper – or sometimes at the margins of it. The field of the history of economic science is a strongly established research field. It investigates the history of economic ideas and arguments, but it is especially concerned with the history and the development of economic *theory*. Often this is connected to debates around who contributed to economic theory and in which way. According to historian of economic thought Marc Blaug, it is mostly economists with historical interests (and often "heterodox economists,") who contribute to the field, suggesting that much history on economic thinking is done by people trained in economics. According to another prominent historian of economic thought, Denis P. O'Brien (2007), training in economics is necessary because acquaintance with economic techniques is a condition for understanding economic analysis. Indeed, ever since the sophisticated usage of mathematics and econometrics became commonplace in economics, it has been increasingly difficult for non-economists to comprehend these highly technical debates. In line with the argument we are unfolding here about the importance of historical context, we should note that economics (political economy) has often had natural science as its scientific (epistemological and methodological) ideal. Ever since the late nineteenth century and the so-called *Methodenstreit* of economics, mainstream economic science has been nomothetic rather than ideographic. That is, it has been concerned with the discovery of laws and regularities rather than with meaning and understanding of individual historical phenomena. It has been concerned with the development of a true science of the economy, which would increasingly be able to explain, and predict, economic facts. This criterion, i.e., the question of which theory does the best job in explaining economic facts, also has consequences when applied to the *history* of economic science. Indeed, economists have often looked at the history of economic thought this way: history is mostly interesting if it can shed light on the improvement of economics as a science, on who was wrong and who was right, and hence still of some use.

While we do not challenge the merits of the history of economic science or of this particular analytical approach to it ("who was right, who was wrong"), we again stress that this book is about the history of economic rationalities, and not about the history of economic science in the way it has traditionally been conceived. The history of economic rationalities we study here through multiple historical case-studies investigates how historical actors or historical discourse make sense and give meaning to "economic life" (Sewell 2010). It thus differs from much history of economic science in two crucial regards.

First, the ambition has been to "widen" the field of economic rationality. Much theorizing or thinking of "the economy" is done in other areas of life as well as by other academics than economists (just think about sociologists such as Max Weber or anthropologists such as Bronislaw Malinowski or Karl Polanyi). While the economic thinking of "great thinkers" such as Thomas Hobbes, John Locke and Karl Marx does appear in this book, our approach has also been to look at the history of economic rationalities in other areas of life than that of the great thinkers. More broadly, we here follow a more recent trend in intellectual history which is about expanding the boundaries of what intellectual historians study when it comes to the where and the when, the kinds of sources, objects or themes of research, and the plurality of actors which can be focused upon (Christiansen 2012, Thorup 2012).

Second, our ambition has been to situate economic rationality in its historical and cultural contexts (Fourcade 2009, Mitchell 1998, Zelizer 2011). As Marieke De Goede suggests in her Foucauldian inspired genealogy of financial discourse, finance is "profoundly cultural" (De Goede 2005, 179). Indeed, social and economic contexts influence historical economic rationalities, including the works of key thinkers. For example, Eve Chiapello's (2007) work on accounting and the birth of the notion of capitalism argues that the historical practice of double entry bookkeeping was nothing but crucial to the development of Marx' theory of capital. Chiapello shifts the attention from the historical link between accounting and capitalism to the intellectual domain, arguing that accounting (double entry bookkeeping) played a key role for the way in which Marx came to understand capital and its ability to accumulate and to abstract from the concrete materialisations of goods and of liquidity (money). We propose to both shift, broaden and contextualize economic rationalities in history as compared to the ways in which history of economic science is traditionally understood.

***

Economists have conquered economics and the debates on economic issues. Not only have they saturated economic talk with numbers, formula and models, they have also established themselves as the only ones to legitimately talk about the economy, take its temperature, interpret its signals, predict its movements and prescribe remedies. Economics has become a field populated only by economists.

Any decent history of economic thought tells a story of how economic reasoning used to be done by theologians, philosophers, statesmen, merchants and others before the professionalization of economics into a discipline. That is an important story to tell in order to historicize the development of the economist as expert and economics as a sphere of its own. The contingency and historical peculiarity of the present way of things is one important lesson that historicizing does, and which whose lessons we are in constant need to reminded of. The history of economic thought does us all a great service, though one suspects it is a lesson for the most part ignored by economists.

This book is comprised of historical case-studies. They differ in terms of their themes, scope, choice of time periods, and choice of specific historical methods for studying past conceptions of economic rationality. But what unites them is the attempt to historicize different aspects of economic rationality.

In this book we ally ourselves with two ways of historicizing economic rationalities. The one is a story of how the development of economics as a specific field of knowledge has borrowed from, been developed within, separated itself from other fields of knowledge, like theology and moral philosophy, or like the inspirations from physics in the nineteenth century, biology and computer science in the twentieth century and now in some quarters behavioral psychology. For example, in Mirowski's (1989) *More Heat Than Light: Economics as Social Physics, Physics as Nature's Economics*, Mirowski investigates the rise of neo-classical economics and the "marginal revolution" in the 1870s. Mirowski's basic claim is that neo-classical economics was reshaping the science of economics by using physics as its scientific ideal. By rigorously applying mathematics, by formalising economic relationships, and by trying to develop a "pure" science, economics would be able to abstract from historical context. Thermodynamics and the idea of a "general equilibrium" were instrumental for the way in which neo-classical economists conceptualised the economy. Mirowski's historical reconstruction is a reconstruction of how neo-classical economics developed as a science, questioning its epistemology and its modelling of the world by placing and conditioning its rise in the intellectual historical context of late nineteenth century physics. It destabilizes the foundations of neo-classical economics by bringing attention to the historical and intellectual contingency of its rise (Mirowski 1994).

The second way of historicizing done in the chapters below is to explore the many ways in which economic talk is spoken outside the field of economics and outside the language of scientific economics. Here we take a starting point in the concept of "everyday economics" developed by economist David F. Ruccio as "economic talk outside the official discipline of economics" (Ruccio 2008, 3; Ruccio and Amariglio 2003). But whereas Ruccio tends to limit it to the ways economic theory and economic analysis are talked about outside the scholarly discipline of economics (that is, how academic knowledge is reflected in the wider world), we are interested in expanding the meaning of everyday economics even further as detailed below. The economy is not only some separate social sphere, but also something we all engage with, articulate and think about. The economic part of life is not only numbers but also arguments, perceptions and actions. And it is not only spoken about in the language of economic science.

Up through history philosophy and theology have contemplated economic issues as parts of their domain of reasoning and evaluating. They have thought about what money is, what interests are and should be, what are benign and malignant economic practices, how does societal and individual concerns align or depart, what are the lines between the public and the private concerns etc. They have discussed the moralities of the market, positive and negative, the dangers of greed, but also about defence of self-interest, "rightly understood," as the French philosopher Alexis de Tocqueville called it in the 1830s. This is an impressive and varied thinking of the economic which is not only historical. It is not only a past economic rationality superseded and left behind during the scientification of the economic into an economics. The two strands of thinking continues to be a lively resource of thinking about what the economic is, what it should be, how to evaluate its effect on society and morals etc. One ignores these modes of thinking at the peril of not understanding why and how people, economists included, evaluate and discourse about their economic behavior.

Another important source of economic reflection is the arts. Think of Shakespeare's *The Merchant of Venice* or Bret Easton Ellis' *American Psycho*. Think of Charles Defoe's depictions of Victorian poverty, or Emile Zola's of financial manipulations, George Orwell's description and discussion of the beggar in *In and Out of Paris and London*, or the glorifications of extravagant riches in much 1990s hip-hop. The arts offer narratives of what happens when humans enter markets, or are turned into properties, when love is monetized. It allows us to play out various "personifications of capital positions," as Marx called it: the miser, for instance, as the embodiment of money's function as a store of value and the spendthrift as the embodiment of its function as circulation of money. Art and the market have always observed each other, and it is not only money and markets that has influenced art. The arts have also been instrumental in shaping our understandings of the market and of market behaviors (Throsby 2001; Velthuis 2005).

A third major source of economic rationality outside economics is the everyday where people need to go to work, raise their kids, shop, vote and all other kinds of mundane activities and where we all constantly narrate about our choices, dilemmas, opportunities and risks, and where we pass on ideas and standards to others. Actually we will argue that there is as much (history of) economic rationality in a common sense saying as in an economic equation. It is definitely more important in how economic matters play out in real life. There is an everyday economic reasoning going on in a daily basis among people, spreading ideas about economic life, developing standards of evaluation – should I choose this or that education, rent or buy a place to life, shift jobs, buy my girlfriend a present etc. – which is the main way that the economy and life meet in practical terms. No one has ever acted on the basis of an economic model as such, but they have acted and are acting on the basis of various ideas about the economy learned far outside the field of economic science (Roscoe 2014; Ruccio 2009).

In all three areas, moral/religious thinking, the arts and everyday life strong notions are developed and evaluated about values, economic, moral, cultural, social, and how those relate to what can be bought and sold with money, why one goes to work, get an education, buys a house, invest one's pension in stocks etc. but also narratives about money relations among family members and friends, about the liberating and demeaning effects of monetarizing interpersonal relations, of how to look upon things of intimate, personal value. Those rationalities are just as economic as GDP, inflation rates and other obvious economics matters.

Economic rationality as developed within economics have marginalized other forms of economic reasoning and thereby removed the economic from the shared world of all of us, but our argument is that the two strands discussed above, the non-economic fields of knowledge influencing the development of economics as well as "everyday economic rationalities," constantly haunt the economics profession as a self-contained, pure science, as well as demonstrating how the economic is a conversation we all take part of, know a lot about, struggle with and about, not just in the language of economic science.

***

This book is structured chronologically. This is not to imply that there is a (teleological) development of economic rationalities, but because each chapter is situated in particular historical contexts and epochs. The chapters in this book thus span across several historical epochs, and, for the sake of introduction, we will briefly here touch upon some of the most salient features of each of these epochs in the history of the Modern West.

As a historical frame, *the Early Modern (1400–1700)* is almost perfectly suited to the study of economic rational*ities*. Given that the concept of economy had not yet manifested itself as political economy, a range of ideas and practices relating to spending, investing, accumulation and lending held a number of rationalities dealing with economy and trade. These ideas were found in many different fields of knowledge from philosophy, across theological sermons and manifests to humanist literature and merchant handbooks. In addition the slow spread of empirical knowledge as a genuine authority informed many of these debates and discussions in the form of, for instance, reports from cartographic expeditions to foreign cultures and the experimental philosophies which together with mathematics spawned new ways of thinking about quality and quantity. If you are particularly interested in the Early Modern period, read Chaps. 2, 3, 4 and 5.

The Enlightenment (ca. 1700–1850) is an all-important period for understanding the trajectory of economic rationalities. From the late seventeenth century onwards, the writings on population, production, money and property in European languages began to intensify. By the middle of the eighteenth century a large number of such works had been translated, reinterpreted and commented upon throughout Europe. The political awareness of international interconnectedness was on the rise in this period, and the characteristics of the accompanying political and economic rationalities continued to pose important questions. In the construction of notions of a "political economy", economic, moral and political arguments moved in between different contexts and geographies, in which they were combined and reformulated. More durable economic beliefs were shaped out of these intense and complex debates. If you are mainly interested in the Enlightenment, read Chaps. 6, 7 and 8.

Significant for *Industrial Modernity (ca. 1850–1970)* is the professionalization of economics as a discipline, as seen in the rise of economics departments at American and in many European universities. Economics and economic thinking became authorities in the public realm during this period. Economic textbooks became major sources of influence on economic thinking and policy-making; economic models, systematic collection of data, and sophisticated calculations of GDP became new ways in which states could keep track of their own and other states' development. Economic language and reasoning has had a lasting influence on public debates, on economic policies and the understandings of the role of markets, state, and democracy, and on peoples' self-understanding. If you are mainly interested in Industrial Modernity, read Chaps. 9 and 10.

In Contemporary society, c. 1970-present, there has been some profound changes to economic thinking often summarized in concepts like globalization, post-fordism, neoliberalism as well as financialization, cognitive capitalism, knowledge economy and others. What seems evident in all those and related concepts are a recognition of change, and possibly of uncertainty, in the basic institutions and practices of contemporary Western societies. The industrial organization of labour and production, the predominantly national economies and economic policies, and the welfare state are no longer obvious, uncontested or maybe even relevant conceptualizations of our time. Instead, we have witnessed a massive shift in authoritative concepts around words like competition, global market, projects, flexibility, capital, innovation, all bearing witness to an ever-extended marketization. If you are mainly interested in Contemporary Society, read Chaps. 11, 12, 13 and 14.

***

In the first chapter of the book Catherine Secretan focuses upon ecclesiastical and theological influences upon early economic thinking in her *From "Permutation of Commodities" to the Praise of "Doux Commerce:" Changes in Economic Rationality In Early Modern Times*. By looking at a range of merchant handbooks she addresses the moral rationalities of trade and bookkeeping. These were important not just from a moral viewpoint but equally so from a rational viewpoint where morals, social status, credibility were tied together in the ledger of the merchant.

Laurens Van Apeldoorn's *"The Nutrition of a Commonwealth:" Hobbes on Science, Politics, and the Economy* revisits Hobbes' economic thinking in *De Cive* and *Leviathan* and argues along Istvan Hont's dismissal of him as an economic thinker. However, rather than providing a reaffirmation of Hont, van Apeldoorn provides some solutions as to Hobbes' ambiguous nature as creator of both a political and materialistic discourse.

Where Laurens Van Apeldoorn focuses upon Hobbes' economic thinking, Christoffer Basse Eriksen's *Circulation of Blood and Money in Leviathan – Hobbes on the Economy of the Body* focuses especially upon Hobbes' use of metaphors and his dependency upon William Harvey. Metaphors played an indispensable role in the development and legitimization of early modern economic rationalities. Hobbes' conception of economy as a closed system of circulation ensuring the health and life of the state was influenced by William Harvey's anatomical theory of the circulation of blood for his description of the state as a body. For Harvey, a proper circulation of blood was what ensured the life of the animal body, and thus for Hobbes the economy understood as circulation of money was nothing but a means to ensure the life of the political body.

Jakob Bek-Thomsen's *Profits and Morals in Leon Battista Alberti's I libri della famiglia* focuses on ideas of growth before the creation of the concept of economic growth. By looking at ideas of progress and accumulation of capital in Late Medieval and Early Renaissance, Bek-Thomsen explores how these ideas were understood as virtuous and beneficial, not only to the individual but also society as a whole. As such, Bek-Thomsen revisits Leon Battista Alberti's book on household economy and provides a new look at Sombart's favorite *bourgeois*. However, rather than reading Alberti as ebodying a capitalist spirit or a civic humanism, Bek-Thomsen takes a closer look at the structural and analytical levels of Alberti's household management.

Campbell Jones' chapter, *The Meanings of Work in John Locke*, argues that there are at least four ideas of work in Locke that fold into one another, contradict one another and in doing so at times support one another. Jones thereby argues against the conventional view that there is in Locke one clear and distinct idea of work. According to Jones, Locke's thought only makes sense if one concedes to it a set of presuppositions of origin, which play out in original unmediated access to the world and to God and a somehow originary labour that sets everything else in train. This idea of pure origin, however, is a religious metaphysics of origin in which the origin is always mysterious and unavailable to us fallen ones who are only of this world.

Niccolò Valmori sheds light on how economic rationalities were part of how global financial systems emerged. In his chapter, *Financial Reasoning in The Midst of Revolution and Wars: Merchants and Bankers Between Paris, London, and Amsterdam,* Valmori explores the economic practices of dominant bankers at the turn of the eighteenth century. A number of different strategies were invented in this era in response to wars and ensuing economic crises. Valmori argues that while bankers would traditionally have national stability as the main component of their economic reasonings, this approach was trumped by visions of diversification in the realm of global finance.

Jill Bradbury investigates the relation between cultural and economic modes of reasoning in the chapter *Prose Genre and the Emergence of Modern Economic Reasoning in Eighteenth-Century Britain.* Bradbury argues that the economic rationalities of early British theories in political economy were dependent on the development of a specific form of prose genre. From the seventeenth century onwards, empiricist scientific discourses were seen as interlinked with questions of rhetorics. This linguistic approach to securing scientific advances became pivotal in eighteenth century writings in political economy. In this manner, Bradbury provides an explanation as to why Adam Smith's *Wealth of Nations* could be received and promoted both as a rhetorical narrative and as piece of scientific evidence.

In the chapter *Political Economy and its Public Contenders 1820–1850*, Stefan Gaarsmand Jacobsen & Thomas Palmelund Johansen investigate how newly founded British and French working class newspapers attacked the idea of a universal science of the economy. The question of basic economic rationalities was at the core of this working class attack on the dominant theories of political economy. Jacobsen and Johansen argue that at the heart of the battle over the scientific status of political economy lay the question whether or not there would always be political and moral notions at play when people from different classes developed basic theories about an economic system. Importantly, these debates were pre-Marxist and showcase an alternative approach to working class economic rationalities than what became dominant in Marxist socialism.

Picking up on rationalities which became dominant in Marxist thought, Mikkel Thorup's chapter *The Promissory Self – Credit and Debt Rationalities in the Work and Life of Karl Marx* studies the experience of the debtor as a key to understanding how moral and economic rationalities interact. Thorup focuses on less studied passages in Marx' letters and manuscripts in order to explain the role of personal engagement with debt in the midst of the theoretical work to dispel capitalist relations altogether.

Mark Bevir's chapter, *A New Governance: Hierarchies, Markets, and Networks, cc. 1979–2010*, focuses on the intellectual sources of the transformation of the state and its relation to civil society. It highlights the role played in this transformation by modernist social science, with its reliance on formal explanations based on economic models or sociological correlations. Modernist social science informed the main narratives of the crisis of the administrative and welfare state in the 1970s. Modernist social science also inspired the two waves of public sector reform that responded to this crisis. In Britain, the first wave of reform was most prominent under Thatcherism, at which time an economic modernism inspired marketization and the new public management. The second wave of reform was most prominent under New Labour, at which time a sociological modernism inspired joined-up governance and networks.

Whereas Bevir's chapter both shows that "The economic concept of rationality found in neoclassical theory has a distinctive history", and how that concept influenced public sector reform in Britain, the next two chapters demonstrates its role in arts and health policies. Erwin Dekker's chapter, *The Economic De-legitimization and Legitimization of Arts Policies 1970–1985*, shows how a neoliberal economic epistemology came to dominate the discourse on stately support to the arts in the Anglo-Saxon world. Dekker traces the clash between a micro-economic rationality that was part of the economics imperialism movement of the postwar period, and the established discourse of arts as an essential part of a civilized society. The economic rationality eventually succeeded in challenging the legitimacy and the extent to which the arts deserved support, but it did so by side-stepping some of the most difficult issues: what is excellence in the arts (by measuring secondary social and economic effects), and what importance should be attached to consumer preferences (by assuming consumer sovereignty).

Katherine E. Kenny's chapter, *From "Health for All" to "Health as Investment:" The Role of Economic Rationalities in the Transition From International to Global Health 1978 – 2013*, examines the role of economic rationalities in the transition from international health to global health since the late 1970s. It focuses, in particular, on the recent rise to prominence of non-communicable diseases (NCDs) on the global health agenda. The chapter contrasts the current era of global health, in which health is imagined as a form of human capital and as a site of investment with a post-war era of international health during which health was advocated as a human right and public good. It argues that the transition can be best understood as resulting from the rise of economic rationalities in the field of world health over the last 25 years.

Where Dekker's and Kenny's chapters focuses upon a neoliberal economic rationality in the contexts of arts and health policies, the next chapter zooms in upon debates about the economic rationality (legitimacy) of corporations in society. Christian Olaf Christiansen's chapter, *The Economic Rationality of "Doing Good To Do Well" and Three Critiques: 1990s To The Present*, explores the recent decades' rapid spreading of a discourse which says that business and profitability can be combined with ethical conduct and social concerns. The idea of combining business with "doing good" can be theorised as a new "spirit" of "civic" capitalism. It embodies two meanings of economic rationality: "doing good" is good (rational) business and, second, the dedifferentiation of business and "doing good" offers a new kind of social legitimacy for business. Christiansen argues that this spirit of civic capitalism draw on at least three types of criticism: a *reality check*, asking whether corporations actually practice what they preach; an *ethical check*, asking about which kinds of ethics is typically assumed in e.g. mainstream CSR or corporate philanthropy; and a *democratic check*, investigating the spread of e.g. CSR in the context of overall distribution of responsibilities between business, state, government and civil society.

***

The case-studies in this volume do not follow a single thread in the history of economic rationalities, but several. But by embracing this diversity, pluralism and the battles and conceptual struggles about economic rationalities, the book highlights the many and interesting aspects about the history of economic rationalities, offering rich chances of comparison, historical self-recollection, and invitations to think further about possible spaces, similarities, and connections between the chapter topics. Sometimes the threads run parallel – as when a particular, neoliberal economic rationality runs into the understandings of arts and health policies at about the same time, in a strikingly powerful manner. Sometimes one thinker leaves a mark which continues to exert its influence on economic rationalities, as when Locke articulated his notion of private property. One thing seems certain: humans will to continue to justify, critique, legitimize, make sense of their economic arrangements, as well as to develop new theories about economics and economic rationality. We hope that by addressing important aspects and steps in the the long, tumultuous and many-sided histories of economic rationalities, we contribute a little to historicize those conceptions of economic rationality which have been dominant in the four last decades and demonstrate that economic rationalities have not historically and is not at present a domain for economists only, but a place where everyone deliberate on how to satisfy needs, distribute just deserts, produce and reproduce the conditions of life.

Bibliography

Barma, N.H., and S.K. Vogel, ed. 2008. *Political Economy Reader: Markets as Institutions*. New York: Routledge.

Blaug, M. 2001. No History of Ideas, Please, We're Economists. *Journal of Economic Perspectives* 15(1): 145–164.

Chiapello, È. 2007. Accounting and the Birth of the Notion of Capitalism. *Critical Perspectives on Accounting* 18: 263–293.

Christiansen, Christian Olaf. 2012. From the "History of Economic Thought" to "Economic Intellectual History". *Ideas in History* 2(6): 11–36.

De Goede, M. 2005. *A Genealogy of Finance: Virtue, Fortune, and Faith*. Minneapolis: University of Minnesota Press.

du Gay, Paul, and Michael Pryke. 2002. *Cultural Economy*. London: Sage.

Fourcade, M. 2009. Economists and Societies. In *Discipline and Profession in the United States, Britain, and France, 1890s to 1990s*. Cambridge: Cambridge University Press.

Galbraith, J.K. 1956. *American Capitalism. Revised ed.* Boston: Houghton Mifflin.

Henderson, W., et al. 1993. *Economics and Language*. London/New York: Routledge.

Klamer, Arjo. 2007. *Speaking of Economics. How To Get in the Conversation*. London/New York: Routledge.

McCloskey, Deirdre. 1985. *The Rhetorics of Economics*. Madison: University of Wisconsin Press.

———. 1990. *If You're So Smart. The Narrative of Economic Expertise*. Chicago: University of Chicago Press.

———. 1994. *Knowledge and Persuasion in Economics*. Cambridge: Cambridge University Press.

———. 2006. *The Bourgeois Virtues. Ethics in an Age of Commerce*. Chicago: University of Chicago Press.

Mirowski, Philip. 1989. *More Heat Than Light: Economics as Social Physics, Physics as Nature's Economics*. Cambridge: Cambridge University Press.

Mirowski, Philip. 1994. *Natural Images in Economic Thought*. Cambridge: Cambridge University Press.

Mitchell, Timothy. 1998. Fixing the Economy. *Cultural Studies* 12(1): 82–101.

O'Brien, D.P. 2007. *History of Economic Thought as an Intellectual Discipline*. Cheltenham/Northampton: Edward Elgar.

Ray, Larry, and Andrew Sayer. 1999. *Culture and Economy After the Cultural Turn*. London: Sage.

Roscoe, Philip. 2014. *I Spend, Therefore I am*. London: Penguin.

Ruccio, David, ed. 2008. *Economic Representations. Academic and Everyday*. London: Routledge.

Ruccio, David. 2009. *Economic Representations, Academic and Everyday*. London/New York: Routledge.

Ruccio, David F., and Jack Amariglio. 2003. *Postmodern Moments in Modern Economics*. Princeton/Oxford: Princeton University Press.

Sandel, Michael. 2012. *What Money Can't Buy. The Moral Limits of Markets*. London: Penguin.

Sewell, W.H. Jr. 2010. A Strange Career: The Historical Study of Economic Life. *History and Theory* 49: 146–166.

Shell, Marc. 1982. *Money, Language and Thought. Literary and Philosophical Economies from the Medieval to the Modern Era*. Berkeley: University of California Press.

Skinner, Q. 2002. Moral Principles and Social Change. In *Visions of Politics*, vol. 1, ed. Quentin Skinner. Cambridge: Cambridge University Press.

Supiot, Alain. 2012. *The Spirit of Philadelphia*. London: Verso.

Thorup, M. 2012. Intellektuel Historie. *Temp* 4: 177–189.

Throsby, David. 2001. *Economics and Culture*. Cambridge: Cambridge University Press.

Velthuis, Olav. 2005. *Imaginary Economics*. Rotterdam: NAI.

Zelizer, V.A. 2011. *Economic Lives: How Culture Shapes the Economy*. Princeton: Princeton University Press.

Chapter 2
From "Permutation of Commodities" to the Praise of "Doux Commerce." Changes in Economic Rationality in Early Modern Times

Catherine Secretan

The Early Modern Times saw a crucial shift in economic rationality. Although political economy as a specific discipline only appeared in the beginning of the eighteenth century, some decisive steps occurred between fifteenth and sixteenth centuries, due to political and social changes. Aristotle, who first developed a scientific discussion on economy (defined as the good running of domestic matters for the well-being of one's family), had formulated, in the Nicomachean Ethics, his conception of economic exchange within an ethical investigation (Aristotle 2009, 85). Attached to the definition of justice, the purpose of exchange was not profit or the desire for gain, but a "just" distribution of goods according to the needs of the individuals: suum cuique. The role of commercial exchange, although essential to the cohesion of society, was understood as part of a system of economic autarchy. Aristotle's insight stood in total contrast to the political function that mercantilism and the emergence of commercial capitalism would confer to economy in the fifteenth and sixteenth centuries. Although important, Aristotle's economic thought was only one of the various textual traditions that influenced scholastic ideas on economy, which remained heavily dependent on ecclesiastical culture and Christian principles. Up until the Renaissance, the pursuit of profit and handling of money were condemned or suspected of being inspired by greed. A change occurred during the Renaissance, with broadening of commercial exchange and the emergence of a new conception of reason of state. While Machiavelli (1469–1527) thought of war as a central issue in politics (Machiavelli 1994, 235–253), Giovanni Botero (1544–1617) gave priority to wealth and the government had to play an economic role to secure its political power (Botero 1990, 201–205). As a consequence of this new

C. Secretan (✉)
Centre National de la Recherche Scientifique, Paris, France
e-mail: catherine.secretan@ens-lyon.fr

J. Bek-Thomsen et al. (eds.), *History of Economic Rationalities*, Ethical Economy 54, DOI 10.1007/978-3-319-52815-1_2

theory, the social status of merchants was raised to a moral pre-eminence and economy was seen as a force of sociability and innovation.

2.1 A Mere "Permutation of Commodities"

Between the fourteenth and fifteenth centuries, a number of Italian authors contributed to the foundation of modern commerce. Their books, known as "pratiche di mercatura", were manuals of various sizes and formats, containing most of the commercial knowledge of the time and kept in mercantile offices or taken to the market place. They provided compilations of all kinds of concrete information covering the whole field of commercial knowledge: legal regulations concerning traffic, synoptic tables for the comparison of weights, measures, currencies, tariffs, price lists, insurance contracts, dates of fairs, local uses and often, a careful description of the main products and specialities to be found in each country. Generally preserved as manuscripts, they were more often printed from the fifteenth century onwards, although they were never meant for the public. Disseminated all over the world of merchants, they constituted the Ars Mercatoria of the time (Hoock et al. 1991) and from the range of places and cities mentioned, they obviously bear witness to a global economy covering the whole of Europe and extending as far as China. One of the most famous of these textbooks was that by Francesco Pegolotti, *Della Decima et delle altre gravezze*, written around 1340 by a Florentine merchant of the powerful Bardi Company, and kept in manuscript until the eighteenth century (Evans 1936). This manual is one of the most complete encyclopaedias of practical mercantile information, providing all kinds of tips needed by merchants travelling as far as China, and giving precise indications about the best road from Europe to "Cathay" (China).

Typical of all merchants' books of this time, Pegolotti's reasoning was purely commercial and practical, with no moral or theoretical concepts, except for one well-known issue: the prohibition of usury. During the Middle Ages, usury was regarded as a sin and was consequently forbidden by the Church (Noonan 1957, 20–25). Since Antiquity, the core maxim was that money does not beget money ("nummus non parit nummos"), although the motives that inspired Greek and Latin authors were not the same as those justifying the Christian condemnation. When taken over by Christian theologians, the prohibition of interest on money became founded on Luke: 6, 35: "Do good, and lend, hoping for nothing again" (Noonan 1957, 346–348). Calvin broke with this tradition of prohibiting the profits of trade and finance and set them "on the same level of respectability as the earning of the labourer and the rents of the landlord" (Tawney 1977, 113). His "Letter on Usury" (1545) was a turning point in fostering a new economic rationality: "I therefore conclude that usury must be judged not by a particular passage of Scripture, but simply by the rules of equity. (…) Therefore, the profit does not arise from that money but from the produce that results from its use or employment" (quoted in Le Van Baumer 1978, 231–233). From then on, the road was clear for credit and money lending.

A new attitude towards commerce appeared in the work of the Venetian merchant Benedetto Cotrugli (1416–1469), *Della mercatura e del mercante perfetto*, first published in Venice in 1573. Cotrugli's book is well known for being one of the first to provide a systematic presentation of accounting and a description of double-entry bookkeeping (Cotrugli 1573, 36–39), a "revolutionary leap into the calculation of profit" (Soll 2014, 11). It is also important for its complete description of commerce, its origin, history, practice and scope: "Commerce, if well considered, has its origin in nature" (Cotrugli 1573, 6). From the qualities required for the "perfect merchant", Cotrugli's book can be seen as a "Mirror for Merchants", based on the model of the many "Mirrors for Princes", a genre much enjoyed at the same time. From honest living to piety, through the full range of liberal arts that he should strive to learn, the merchant is given a new status and becomes representative of a new social class (Jacob and Secretan 2008, 147). The parallel with the book by Cotrugli's contemporary, Leon Battista Alberti (1404–1472) *I libri della famiglia*, published in 1434 – although much more developed than Cotrugli's book – illustrates this emergence of a new social group, distinct from the nobility and praised for its capacity of innovation and self-creating independence (Tenenti 1978, 124–125). One of the main characteristics of Cotrugli's manual also concerns the claim for theory. In the dedication to a famous merchant of Ragusa, there is a significant passage in which Cotrugli says that commerce is missing a "doctrine" and he complains about the disorganised state of commerce: "Ora nell'arte di mercantia io trovai il culto inetto, disordinato, dissoluto, & vano, intanto, che mi indusse à compassione, e dolsimi, che questa arte tanto necessaria, di tanto bisogno, si opportuna, & utile, fosse prevenuta in mano de gl'indotti & rozi huomini, & governata senza modo, senza ordine, con abuso, & senza leggi" (Cotrugli 1573, 2). Then, after arguing about the general value of reasoning, either by induction or by deduction from practice to theory and to nature, he set out to built a theory of the art of commerce ("dar dottrina"), that is to say to "reduce it to art": "E perche di questa arte, si naturale, si necessaria, & si utile, non si truova alcun precetto scritto, io similmente con silentio me ne passeria, se mediante la prattica, ch'io ho deldetto esercitio, non havessi inteso che ella si puo ridurre in arte, & massimamente per quello, che usano tutto'l giorno li mercanti di nostra età" (Cotrugli 1573, 7). This expression, together with the complaint about the disorderly state of commercial knowledge, is a remarkable sign of Cotrugli's shared feeling with the scholars of his time about teaching and his commitment to the Humanist reform movement (Gilbert 1960, 69). Cotrugli's manual is one of the best examples of the "discursive broadening" that characterized merchants' manuals in the early modern period (Jacob and Secretan 2008, 147).

2.2 Utilitarian Conversion: Economy as Part of Politics

When Jacques Savary (1622–1690), a Frenchman who worked for Finance Minister Colbert, published his famous book *Le parfait négociant* (1675), partly taking up Cotrugli's title, the providential character he ascribed to commerce could be seen as reflecting the utilitarian turn of economic rationality. "De la manière que la Providence de Dieu a disposé les choses sur la terre, on voit bien qu'il a voulu establir l'union et la charité entre tous les hommes, puisqu'il leur a imposé une espèce de necessité d'avoir toujours besoin les uns des autres" (Savary 1675, 1). This mutual help with regard to individual welfare was extended to the individual's relation to the state in the changing conception of a well governed society. Citizen participation in government was no longer conceived as "simply civic or virtuous" (Pocock 2003, 436), but as an economic participation in a new system in which trade became crucial to the state's safety. In opposition to Machiavelli, who based the state's safety on war, or at least on the fear of war, Giovanni Botero considered the wealth of a state to be its strongest power. The theoretic framework for his idea was inspired by the expansion of a new monetary system, that of mercantilism to which foreign trade (and hence, national industry and commerce) was central in creating abundance of money. Botero therefore entrusted political authority with economic responsibility in such issues as those of money, population, and industry. Such a new conception, which promoted solidarity between private and public interests – as subsequently theorized by Adam Smith (1723–1790), in particular – implied a radical shift in economic rationality and should be considered as one of the first signs of the emergence of political economy (Senellart 1989, 90).

Although creating the expression of "political economy" and choosing it as a title for his treatise published in 1615, *Traicté de l'économie politique*, Antoine de Montchrétien (1575–1621) did not invent economy as a specific science, but his book, dedicated to the regent Marie de Medici, and her son Louis XIII, is a meaningful step in the changing realities. By presenting profit as a legitimate aim in private well-being (Montchrétien 1999, 63–67) and wealth as a component of political power (Montchrétien 1999, 279–280), he followed the line of this "utilitarian conversion" to which Hobbes' anthropology will give a theoretical consecration by defining self-interest as directed towards self-preservation. In his treatise on *De Cive* (On the Citizen) (1642), Hobbes made individual desire for profit a natural and rightful passion, hence a citizen's right which is incumbent on the political authority to respect: "Sovereign can do no more for the citizens' happiness than to enable them to enjoy the possessions their industry has won them, safe from foreign and civil war" (Hobbes 1998, 144).

2.3 The Praise of "Doux Commerce"

Within the new reason of state and the development of mercantilism, trade was attributed, in Early Modern Times, a political and socializing function, which neither Aristotle nor Machiavelli – for very different reasons – would ever have thought of. This consecration was given by Montesquieu (1689–1755) who wrote, in *De l'esprit des lois*, about the "sweetness of mores" that trade, in his view, could generate: "C'est presque une règle générale, que partout où il y a des mœurs douces, il y a du commerce, et que partout où il y a du commerce, il y a des mœurs douces"

(Montesquieu 1748, 2). But the premises of such a liberal paradigm can already be found in a book entitled *Il Negotiante*, written by a learned merchant of Genoa, Giovanni Domenico Peri (1590–1666), published in 1638. This text placed emphasis on the generic meaning of the word "trade" ("Negotio"). The author noted that merchants' practice used to lend the general term of the profession to all kinds of mutual relations between human beings – and went as far as to describe human devotion as a "spiritual trade" (Peri 1672, 1). Giovanni Domenico Peri also considered the glory of commerce to be similar to that provided by soldiering or literature. From the very first lines of his book, he wrote: "Tutti gli Huomini devono aspirare all'acquisto delle Virtù, dalle quali vien partorita la Gloria; e fra le molte vie, che a questa conducono, tre specialmente sono le più communi. L'una dell'armi, l'altra delle Lettere, e questa de' Negotij. La prima è pericolosa, la seconda quieta, e la terza faticosa" (Peri 1672, 1). Throughout the "Proemio" of his book, and several times later in the book, Giovanni Domenico Peri praises the merchant's industry. His concept of strain and tireless effort, seen as both a necessity and a virtue, is a remarkable premonition of the value ascribed to "labour" by classical political economy (see Larrère 1992).

Il Negotiante reflects the new vision of merchant activity. Only 6 years later, it very faithfully echoed what the famous Dutch scholar Caspar Barlaeus (1584–1648) had expressed in his oration of 1632. To celebrate the creation of the Athenaeum Illustre of Amsterdam and the chair of Philosophy to which he had just been appointed, Barlaeus pronounced an inaugural discourse entitled *Mercator Sapiens* (1632), "The Learned Merchant" (Secretan 2002). This praise of the merchant's virtues was mainly intended for an audience composed of merchant bankers and big entrepreneurs rather than a public of ordinary trading men. This discourse reflected the city's leading position as a colonial market, money centre and a famous place for the teaching of accounting and publishing. Replacing Antwerp after the fall of the city in 1585, Amsterdam had acquired a great mastery in double-entry bookkeeping. It was from here that Luca Pacioli's accounting manual, *De computis* (printed in 1494) (Soll 2014, 48–54), would be disseminated throughout Europe and first translated (into Dutch). From the late fifteenth century, many merchant schools were created throughout the country (Leiden, Delft, Gouda, Rotterdam, Middelburg, and Utrecht). Therefore, more than any other city in Early Modern Europe, Amsterdam was the place where economic rationality and new banking techniques acquired their full meaning and visibility (see Lesger 2006). The political dimension of foreign trade, in particular, was seen as fundamental to the Republic's power and supremacy. It inspired all defences of national policy, starting with John de Witt's *True Interest and Political Maxims of the Republick of Holland and West Friesland* (1702) (Wilson 1978, 11; Boxer 1966).

Barlaeus' *Mercator Sapiens* is also revealing of changing cultural realities, in that it promotes a secular vision of trade in general. Arguing from the polysemy of the word "commerce" – exactly as did Giovanni Domenico Peri, quoted above – Barlaeus developed a metaphor implying that commercial activity is the true pattern of all human exchanges and the best tool for sociability (Hirschman 1977, 60–61). Thus, as he says, Amsterdam is the city where "merchants buying and selling worldly goods and those selling spiritual food, science and arts" (Secretan 2002, 129) continuously meet. Barlaeus' discourse was obviously meant to serve merchants' interest and consequently provides a new vision of economic rationality and value, according to which the merchant has become not only a "self-acting" individual, but the paradigmatic embodiment of all kinds of exchange, material as well as spiritual: "How fortunate is the city of Amsterdam where merchants may practice Philosophy and Philosophers may practice trade" (Secretan 2002, 165). According to this view, the merchant appears as the cosmopolitan man par excellence: his knowledge in all fields of human learning and his travels throughout the entire world, are factors that raise him to the status of an advocate of tolerance and a hero of human exchange. He constitutes the best representative of a city that attracts both commodities and men from all over the world (Secretan 2002, 80).

2.4 Conclusion

Apart from the hermeneutic virtue of a Weberian approach (Weber 1958), studying the changing views on the social status and self-image of merchants can throw new light on the meaning of modern economic rationality. Early printed merchant textbooks were not concerned with moral and ethical considerations on the role of merchants and their contribution to social welfare, as the scope of these manuals mainly consisted of providing practical knowledge about mercantile activity. A transformation occurred with theorization of mercantile rules and replacement of handbooks by encyclopaedias and "Dictionaries of commerce". This transformation was actually the result of a changing view on the theory of the state and the political dimension ascribed to commerce, money and industry in all aspects concerning state safety threatened by international rivalries. As a consequence of this new vision, self-interest was hailed as able to contribute to public welfare and was adopted by Philosophy as a socially useful passion. The merchant "perfection", although still presented in the style of the traditional "Mirror for merchant" genre, was given a completely different meaning, as best illustrated by the Dutch eulogy discourse of Barlaeus. Discarding the negative – or at least restrictive – Christian ethic of the late Middle Ages, a new interpretation introduced secular praise of merchants' reasonable strive for individual interest as both paradigmatic of all kinds of human exchange and an incentive to self-creative individual autonomy.

Bibliography

Aristotle. 2009. *The Nicomachean Ethics*. Trans. David Ross. Oxford: Oxford University Press.

Barlaeus, Caspar. 2002. *Le 'Marchand philosophe' de Caspar Barlaeus. Un éloge du commerce dans la Hollande du Siècle d'Or,* Trans. Catherine Secretan. Paris: Champion.

Botero, Giovanni. 1990. In *Della ragion di stato e Delle cause della grandezza delle città [1598]*, ed. Luigi Firpo. Bologna: A. Forni.

Boxer, Charles R. 1966. *The Dutch Seaborne Empire*. 1600–1800. London: Hutchinson.

Coornhert, Dirk. 1630. *Werken*. T'Amsteldam, By Iacob Aersz. Colom.

Evans, Allan. 1936. *La pratica della mercatura*. Cambridge, MA: Mediaeval Academy of America.

Gilbert, Neal Ward. 1960. *Renaissance Concepts of Method*. New York: Columbia University Press.

Hirschman, Albert O. 1977. *The Passions and the Interests: Political Arguments for Capitalism Before Its Triumph*. Princeton: Princeton University Press.

Hobbes, Thomas. 1998. *On the Citizen*, ed. Richard Tuck. Trans. Michael Silverthorne. Cambridge, MA: Cambridge University Press.

Hoock, Jochen, Pierre Jeannin, et al., eds., 1991. *Ars Mercatoria. Eine analytische Bibliographie*, 3 vols. Paderborn: Schöningh.

Jacob, Margaret C., and Catherine Secretan, eds., 2008. *The Self-Perception of Early Modern Capitalists*. New York: Palgrave-Macmillan.

Larrère, Catherine. 1992. *L'invention de l'économie au XVIIIe siècle*. Paris: Presses Universitaires de France.

Le Van Baumer, Francis. 1978. *Main Currents of Western Thought: Reading in Western European Intellectual History from the Middle Ages to the Present*. Yale: Yale University Press.

Lesger, Clé. 2006. *The Rise of the Amsterdam Market and Information Exchange: Merchants, Commercial Expansion and Change in the Spatial Economy of the Low Countries c.1550–1630*. London: Ashgate.

Machiavelli, Niccolo. 1994. In *De Principatibus [1532]*, ed. Giorgio Inglese. Roma: Istituto Storico Italiano per il Medio Evo.

Montchrétien, Antoine de. 1999. In *Traicté de l'oeconomie politique*, ed. François Billacois. Genève: Droz.

Montesquieu, Charles Louis de Secondat, baron de. 1748. *De l'esprit des lois*. Genève.

Noonan, John Thomas. 1957. *The Scholastic Analysis of Usury*. Harvard: Harvard University Press.

Peri, Giovanni Domenico. 1672. *Il Negotiante*. Venetia: Presso Gio. Giacomo Hertz.

Pocock, J.G.A. 2003 (1st ed. 1975). *The Machiavellian Moment. Florentine Political Thought and the Atlantic Republican Tradition*. Princeton: Princeton University Press.

Senellart, Michel. 1989. *Machiavélisme et raison d'état: XIIe-XVIIIe siècle*. Paris: Presses Universitaires de France.

Soll, Jacob. 2014. *The Reckoning: Financial Accountability and the Rise and Fall of Nations*. New York: Allen Lane, Basic Books.

Tawney, Richard. 1977 (1st ed. 1926). *Religion and the Rise of Capitalism*. Penguin Books: London.

Tenenti, Alberto. 1978. *Credenze, ideologie, libertinismi tra Medioevo ed età moderna*. Bologna: Il Mulino.

Weber, Max. 1958 (1st ed. 1902). *The Protestant Ethic and the Spirit of Capitalism*. New York: Scribner.

Wilson, Charles. 1978. *Profit and Power. A Study of England and the Dutch Wars*. The Hague/Boston/London: Martinus Nijhoff.

Witt, John de. 1702. *True Interest and Political Maxims of the Republick of Holland and West Friesland*. London.

Chapter 3
"The Nutrition of a Commonwealth:" On Hobbes's Economic Thought

Laurens van Apeldoorn

3.1 Introduction

Hobbes has an equivocal legacy as economic thinker.[1] On the one hand commentators point out that there is hardly any place for the economy in his political philosophy. We find in his work no sustained effort to provide an account of the economic institutions needed for a flourishing state. As Istvan Hont observes in *Jealousy of Trade*, "It is practically pure politics" (Hont 2010, 2). Accordingly, in histories of the development of the discipline of political economy in the seventeenth and eighteenth centuries he is often allotted a marginal role if he is mentioned at all (Eg. Hirschmann 1977; Appleby 1978; Force 2003; Taylor 2010). On the other hand Hobbes has continued to fascinate those aiming to understand the development of economic thought in the early modern period. C.B. Macpherson, for instance, identifies him as an early apologist of the modern capitalist order in which "market relations … shape or permeate all social relations" (MacPherson 1962, 48). Hobbes's account of human nature seems to capture the bourgeois morality of self-interest and unbridled material accumulation. Others add that while he never conceived of the market as a self-regulating mechanism he did contribute to the development

[1]Abbreviations and editions of Hobbes's works used: L: *Leviathan*, ed. Noel Malcolm. Oxford: Oxford University Press, 2012; DCv: *On the Citizen*, ed. Richard Tuck and Michael Silverthorne. Cambridge: Cambridge University Press, 1998; EL: *The Elements of Law*, ed. Ferdinand Tönnies. London: Frank Cass & Co, 1969. References are to book (if applicable), chapter and paragraph, and include page numbers.

Versions of this paper were presented at 'Scientiae: Disciplines of knowing in the early modern world' (Vienna, 2014) and 'Economic rationalities: economic reasoning as knowledge and practice authority' (Aarhus, 2014). I would like to thank audiences at those conferences, and in particular Jakob Bek-Thomsen, for helpful comments.

L. van Apeldoorn (✉)
Leiden University, Anna van Buerenplein 301, 2595 DG The Hague, The Netherlands
e-mail: L.C.J.van.Apeldoorn@phil.leidenuniv.nl

J. Bek-Thomsen et al. (eds.), *History of Economic Rationalities*, Ethical Economy 54, DOI 10.1007/978-3-319-52815-1_3

classical economic thought by conceiving human motivation and value as based on self-interest (Langholm 1998, 151), and that he explicates "the basic premises underlying rational-choice analyses of human behaviour" (McArthur 2012, 178–79) which are at the heart of so much of contemporary economic theory. Moreover, commentators take note of some of his suggestive assertions regarding the way in which the economic realm should be organised (Eg. Levy 1954). For instance, Hobbes seems to accept that prices must be determined on the basis of agreement of buyer and seller, since there is no objective measure of value over and above the preferences of individuals, and he defends apparently far-reaching economic freedom for individuals to pursue their interests through economic transactions (L 21.7, p. 330, cf. DCv. 13.6, p. 144). Furthermore, since he seems to limit the functions of the state to the provision of peace and defence one commentator goes as far as maintaining that the "sovereign is there, in fact, to remove certain standing obstacles to the secure prosecution by his subjects of their individual aims" and thus that "Hobbes may be regarded as a forerunner of the negative *laisser aller* doctrine" (Taylor 1908, 101).

Although Hobbes's ambiguous status as an economic thinker has been noted before, to my knowledge no attempt has yet been made to explain what features of his thought may have given rise to it. In this chapter I aim to trace these seemingly incongruent assessments of his philosophy to the nature and application of his scientific method. In Sect. 3.2, I argue that there are two features of his method that should be of particular interest to those concerned with the historical development of the field of economics. First, Hobbes is arguably the first who embraces what has become known as methodological individualism, the view that social phenomena should be studied by reference to the dispositions and actions of individuals (Lukes 1968, 119). Secondly, his study of the motivations and dispositions of individuals bears more than a passing resemblance to the *homo economicus* that populates much of modern microeconomics. Nevertheless, he does not directly apply his method to economic phenomena. In Sect. 3.3, I show why economic questions always have political answers. Hobbes develops above all a *political* science, almost exclusively focussing on the political institutions that must be established for peace to be maintained and human flourishing to be possible. Finally, in Sect. 3.4, I explain why this is the case. While Hobbes in later work comes to realise that he must provide an account of the "art of government" related to the material conditions of the commonwealth, and makes some attempts to offer a guide to government policy in the domain of the economy, he fails to properly integrate these observations into his political science. The use of a pervasive metaphor of the commonwealth as "body politic" to structure these observations prevents him from grounding his reflections on economic governance in his scientific method and conception of human nature. Thus, while he may be credited as having been one of the first to have developed a science of politics, he never did the same for economics.

3.2 Human Nature and Methodological Individualism

Hobbes derives both the need for and shape of a commonwealth or political association from an account of the general dispositions of individuals. In the revised version of *De Cive* he gives a clear outline of his method.

> I should begin with the matter of which a commonwealth is made and go on to how it comes into being and the form it takes, and to the first origin of justice. For a thing is best known from its constituents. As in an automatic Clock or other fairly complex device, one cannot get to know the function of each part and wheel unless one takes it apart, and examines separately the material, shape and motion of the parts, so in investigating the right of a commonwealth and the duties of its citizens, there is a need, not indeed to take the commonwealth apart, but to view it as taken apart, i.e., to understand correctly what human nature is like, and in what features it is suitable and in what unsuitable to construct a commonwealth, and how men who want to grow together must be connected (DCv Preface, p. 10).

In order to provide an account of the appropriate institutions of the commonwealth we must first know the dispositions of individuals. In *De Cive* he simply posits two such principles "well known to all men by experience" (DCv Preface, p. 10), without further defending them. In *Elements of Law* and *Leviathan* (as in *De Homine*) Hobbes develops a more or less complete mechanical psychology that is consistent with his materialistic-deterministic ontology and from which general conclusions may be drawn about "those qualities of man-Kind, that concern their living together in Peace, and Unity" (L 11.1, p. 150). This psychology is sometimes taken to include a form of (predominant) egoism, which is not unreasonable given Hobbes's repeated emphasis, also in his later work, that "of all Voluntary Acts, the Object is to every man his own Good" (L 15.16, p. 230), which indeed suggests that Hobbes takes individuals to display at least a predominant concern for their own well-being (Eg. Kavka 1986). From this account of human motivation he draws a number of general conclusions regarding human dispositions, and in particular attributes to individuals a "perpetuall and restlesse desire of Power after power, that ceaseth onely in Death" (L 11.2, p. 150), a desire "of Ease, and sensuall Delight," and an overwhelming fear of death (L 11.4, p. 152).

These dispositions form the basis for his argument establishing both the possibility and the necessity of entering into a political association. He presents these conclusions of his political science as principles or dictates of reason, also called the laws of nature. These laws are derived from the "known naturall Inclinations of Mankind" (L Review and Conclusion, p. 1139) and outline what individuals must do to enduringly establish a peaceful society. On the one hand, in the state of nature where there is no powerful sovereign to keep individuals in awe, their passions and dispositions will lead them inevitably to war. Indeed, he maintains that nothing less than an absolute sovereign is necessary to counteract the unsociable dispositions of men that lead them to revolt and war. On the other hand, he shows the possibility of creating a stable association, since "all men, by necessity of their nature, want to get out of that miserable and hateful state, as soon as they recognize its misery" (DCv, Preface, p. 12). Their passions are such that they are willing to submit to a sovereign that is dictated by his theory.

Hobbes thus purports to derive the political institutions necessary for human flourishing from "what human nature is like," from the passions and dispositions of the individuals that would populate the commonwealth. This amounts to what in recent times has become known as methodological individualism (Lukes 1968). He provides an analysis of the institutions of the commonwealth and what he conceives as the only realistic alternative, the state of nature, as the aggregate of the many individual actions of individuals which in turn are the result of their dispositions that may perhaps be ultimately reduced to the fundamental desire for their "own Good" (L 15.16, p. 230). Hobbes here reveals a certain affinity with those economists that laid the groundwork for orthodox economic theory in the late nineteenth century, such as Stanley Jevons and F.Y. Edgeworth. These economists develop mathematical systems to model economic phenomena in which they draw on basic principles about the individual psychology. In the words of Jevons, economics aims to "investigate the condition of a mind, and bases upon this investigation the whole of economics" (Quoted in Udehn 2001, 50). In particular they embrace the principle that all agents pursue their "self-interest" as first principle of the discipline. Like Hobbes they attempt to calculate the aggregate of the actions of individuals with certain dispositions given the constraints within which they act. In this sense these theorists are closer to Hobbes than to Adam Smith, whose *Wealth of Nations* (1776) usually is considered to have inaugurated the economic discipline. Smith explicitly rejects that the humans are only moved by self-interest in favour of a more subtle account of human dispositions and is much less than Hobbes drawn to treating the sciences in analogy with the physical sciences as a system of strict deduction (See eg. Force 2003; Fleischacker 2004).

3.3 Political Science

Nevertheless, Hobbes limits his scientific method to political institutions and never subjects economic phenomena to such a scientific analysis. The conclusion of his analysis of human nature is that it is necessary for individuals to submit virtually unconditionally to the authority of a sovereign. He conceives the resulting political association or commonwealth as essentially a set of juridical relations (of right and obligation). That is to say that a commonwealth exists if and only if the rights of sovereignty exist. This is most evident in *Leviathan* where he claims that the rights of sovereignty "make the Essence of Soveraignty" (L 18.16, p. 278) and "in him [i.e., the sovereign] consisteth the Essence of the Common-wealth" (L 17.13, p. 260). On this basis one may conclude that rights of sovereignty form the essence of the commonwealth. Indeed, Hobbes summarises the first two parts of *Leviathan* as accomplishing the derivation of "the Rights of Soveraigne Power, and the duty of Subjects" (L 32.1, p. 576). These obligations are artificial or contractual, in the sense that they come into being through the willed agreement of individuals who are formerly unbound by such obligations (L 18.1, p. 264). In order to create a commonwealth they must contract with one another to let themselves be governed by the sovereign. The covenant brings life to the commonwealth because it creates the juridical relations of right and obligation associated with sovereign power.

Since his premises require him to defend an absolute sovereign, Hobbes cannot bestow on the economy organising principles that are independent of political dictates. This is clear, for instance, from his views on the regulation of property. From the first expression of his political philosophy in *Elements of Law*, circulated in 1640, onwards he maintains that the existence of all property depends on the state. He writes for instance that "before the institution of sovereign power *meum* and *tuum* implied no propriety, but a community, where every man had right to every thing, and was in state of ware with every man" (EL 2.8.8, p. 174). In the state of nature there can be no property because one is constantly liable to violent invasion of all others. From this follows that all economic questions have fundamentally political answers. The organisation of the economy, the system of ownership and production, the distribution of property rights and the rules according to which property can and should be exchanged, all are subject to, and dependent on the absolute authority of the sovereign. Thus, the relationship between, on the one hand, the premises of his account of human nature and his scientific method, and on the other hand his economic views must necessarily be indirect and mediated by his politics. Coordination and cooperation are always dependent on the power and legislative authority of the sovereign.

This, I take it, is Istvan Honts explanation as to why for Hobbes there is hardly any room for the consideration of economic questions in his philosophy. Hobbes's politics is "anticommercial," Hont maintains, because Hobbes focuses all his energies on avoiding the state of nature as the result of his denial that man is a "naturally social or political being." He denies "the political efficacy of natural sociability ... including the utilitarian bonds created by commercial reciprocity" (Hont 2010, 20). Given his dim view of human nature Hobbes is unable to see how order could be attained without an absolutist state. Social order can only be established by political means. Accordingly he refuses to consider the economy as an important consideration in politics and does not include "in his political theory a need-based concept of commercial society as a secondary cause of state formation" (Hont 2010, 43).

The argument establishes that the economic realm, insofar as it supports state formation, must be the object of government policy: economics belongs to the "art of government." However, it does not fully explain why Hobbes does not apply his scientific method to economic questions. As he notes in *Elements of Law*, it is not his aim to "enter into the particulars of the art of government, but to sum up the general heads, wherein such art is to be employed, and in which consisteth the duty of him or them that have sovereign power" (EL 2.9.1, p. 179). Accordingly, he makes some very brief and general observations about relevant responsibilities of the sovereign based on the dictum that "*Salus populi suprema lex*" (EL 2.9.1, p. 179). Since the good of the people consists, among other things, in "Commodity of living" (EL 2.9.3, p. 179), and commodity of living consists in "liberty and wealth" (EL 2.9.4, p. 180) he suggests that the "well ordering of trade, procuring of labour, and forbidding the superfluous consuming of food and apparel" are "in sovereign authority" (EL 2.9.4, p. 180). In *De Cive* he similarly notes that for the citizens' prosperity there are three things necessary: "*products of earth and water, hard work* and *thrift*" (DCv 14.13, p. 150), and maintains not just that the sovereign has authority to legislate on these issues but that they are the objects of "sovereign's duty" (DCv 14.13, p. 150). The sovereign ought to devise laws that promote agriculture, fishing, and industry, and prohibit idleness and the "extravagant expenditure on food and clothes" (DCv 14.13, p. 150). However, more generally the sovereign "can do no more for citizens' happiness than to enable them to enjoy the possessions their industry has won them, safe from foreign and civil war" (DCv 13.6, p. 144). While Hobbes thus notes in these early works that a flourishing commonwealth requires certain material conditions that must be maintained by sovereign action, he apparently does not think it necessary to apply his scientific method in aid of concrete and precise instructions for appropriate legislation.

3.4 The Nutrition of a Commonwealth

In what follows I wish to provide an explanation as to why Hobbes did not integrate economic governance into his political science. One should start by recalling that on his view the essence of the commonwealth consists of a set of rights and obligations. A perfect commonwealth exists when all individuals have submitted (and have recognized to have submitted) their will and judgment to the sovereign in the way outlined by Hobbes in the contract argument. Scientific knowledge in the realm of politics therefore consists of knowledge of the rights of sovereignty and duties of subjects. However, in order to know what rights and duties individuals have it is not necessary to know anything about the material conditions of their lives, that is, whether they have access to food, cloths, shelter and other means to commodious living. Due to this conception of political science as consisting only of knowledge of juridical relations of right and obligation there may be a tendency to ignore the role of material production as essential for the maintenance of the state.

This tendency is visible, for instance when Hobbes in *Elements of Law* discusses taxation and comes close to equating citizens' *obligation* to obey the sovereign with the sovereign being able to acquire the *resources* he demands of them. The defense of a state, he writes, requires "the obedience and unity of the subjects … in which consisteth the means of levying soldiers, and of having money, arms, ships, and fortified places in readiness for defence" (EL 2.9.9, p. 184). If citizens are obedient and act in accordance with the commands of the sovereign, he seems to suggest, resources such as soldiers, money, arms, and ships can be at any moment employed in aid of the defense of the state. This is, of course, is rather too quick. While the conscription of soldiers may perhaps be solely dependent on their obedience, money, arms, and ships require a complex system of material production that cannot be secured by simple command. This is not a structural weakness in his theory, though. I have already noted that Hobbes introduces the governance of the economy in his account of political science as a set of duties of sovereignty. The good of the people should be the aim of sovereign action; sovereigns ought to do what they can "to ensure that the citizens are abundantly provided with all the good things necessary not just for life but for the enjoyment of life" (DCv 8.4, p. 144). This should lead one to wonder why Hobbes says so little about what these duties precisely are.

From *Elements of Law* onwards, Hobbes shows himself to be above all concerned with the problem of order from the perspective of citizens who do not correctly perceive their own obligations and benefit. In *Leviathan* he maintains that it is his aim to "set before mens eyes the mutuall Relation between Protection and Obedience" (L Review and Conclusion, p. 1141). Accordingly, he spends considerable energy defending the practically absolute obligation of citizens to obey any sovereign that is capable of reliably securing their peace and safety. When writing *Elements of Law* and *De Cive* Hobbes must have thought that the corresponding duties of sovereignty, including the duty to promote citizens' commodious living, were less contentious and urgent to require an elaborate treatment.

This changes in *Leviathan*. In *Leviathan* Chapter 24 on "the Nutrition and Procreation of a Commonwealth," Hobbes significantly expands a discussion of the material conditions of state formation that were in embryonic form present in the earlier works, which gives a clear indication that he came to see the need to engage more forcefully with issues concerning economic policy. This is may be due to both shifting concerns and shifting audiences from the early *Elements* and *De Cive* to *Leviathan*. In the latter work Hobbes puts additional emphasis on the importance of "peaceable, sociable, and comfortable living" (L 15.40, p. 242) besides the avoidance of violent conflict, and treats resolving such conflict as necessary precondition for comfortable living. *Leviathan* may also have a different intended audience. Noel Malcolm has recently suggested that *Leviathan* could have been written for Prince Charles (future King Charles II) when Hobbes tutored him in mathematics when they were both exiled in Paris in 1646–48. Malcolm maintains that "overall, the first half of *Leviathan* contains significantly more material than might be placed under the heading "advice to princes" than either of its predecessor texts" (Malcolm 2012, 56). In particular he suggests that Hobbes's use of an extended metaphor, comparing the commonwealth to a human body, which is first introduced in *Leviathan*, may be "designed to capture the interest of, and at the same time to entertain" (Malcolm 2012, 58) the future King. In this context it is notable that Chapter 24 of Leviathan on "the Nutrition and Procreation of a Commonwealth," is entirely couched in terms of this metaphor. It addresses the task of the sovereign to make good "distributive laws" and so to aid the health and wellbeing of the commonwealth. New in these passages are a number of specific claims about the way in which the economy ought to be organised, in aid of the "Distribution of the Nourishment, to the severall Members of the Common-wealth" (L 174). For instance, he maintains that for the "Sustentation of a Commonwealth," it is "necessary that men distribute that which they can spare, and transferre their propriety therein mutually one to another, by exchange, and mutual contract." New is too the emphasis on the circulation of money, which he describes as

> passeth from Man to Man, within the Common-wealth; and goes round about, Nourishing (as it passeth) every part thereof; In so much as this Concoction, is as it were the Singuification of the Common-wealth: For naturall Bloud is in like manner made of the

> fruits of the Earth; and circulating, nourisheth by the way, every Member of the Body of Man (L 24.11, p. 394).

Hobbes here echoes a discussion of the vital motions in the human body that "begun in generation, and continued with interruption through their whole life; such as are the *course* of the *Bloud*, the *Pulse*, the *Breathing*, the *Concoction*, *Nutrition*, *Excretion*, &c. to which motions there needs no help of the Imagination" (L 6.1, p. 78). It is in the context of this extended metaphor of society as living body that leads him to consider advice for the prince as to the appropriate organisation of the economy to guarantee the material conditions of the commonwealth.

This late addition nevertheless remains poorly integrated in the overall structure of his science of politics. This can be shown by comparing the organisation of the economy with other policy questions of relevance to the Hobbesian sovereign, such as importantly the management of the legal system, including legislation, adjudication, and enforcement. These functions are discussed in terms of "dictates of reason," that is, as (implications of) natural law. In chapter 30 of *Leviathan*, titled "Of the OFFICE of the Soveraign Representative," Hobbes notes a number of duties of sovereignty. For instance, it is required of the sovereign that "Justice be equally administred to all degrees of People," in which "consisteth Equity; to which, as being a Precept of the Law of Nature" (L 30.15, p. 534). This refers to the eleventh law of nature, which outlines the requirement of "Equity" or the "Justice of an Arbitrator" (L 15.15, p. 230). Similarly Hobbes notes that the sovereign has a duty to "make a right application of Punishments" which refers to the seventh law of nature which requires that punishments are only employed in aid of the "correction of the offender, or direction of others" (L 15.19, p. 232). These duties can plausibly be understood as forming an integral part of his science of politics since they are, at least in theory, derived by means of certain reasoning from indubitable premises about human nature and the dispositions of man.

But his account of economic governance is not included in the discussion of the laws of nature. Rather it is prompted by the metaphor of the commonwealth as human body. This means that Hobbes does not relate the fundamental principles of his philosophy, including those that some commentators have associated with rational choice theory, to conclusions about the appropriate organisation of material production in society. The analogy between the human and political body may be evocative, but the mode of argument does not conform to his account of scientific method in which conclusions about the appropriate social institutions are derived from a consideration of the aggregate of the many actions individuals given determinate constraints.

3.5 Conclusion

Hobbes's late venture into the realm of economics shows that he was not just narrowly concerned with the nature of political institutions but was willing to consider broader questions of governance in terms of the duties of sovereignty. He should therefore not be faulted for failing to include "economics" as independent science in his classification of forms of knowledge and neither should this fact, by itself, be taken to say anything about Hobbes's attitude to economics (as Taylor 2010, 430 apparently does). He makes questions of the "nutrition of a commonwealth" subordinate to politics, but this is to be expected. He conceives of any institutional organisation to be impossible without the existence of an absolute sovereign, and he accordingly takes the governance of the economy to be the task of a legislator.

I think this explains the equivocal nature of Hobbes's legacy as economic thinker. It explains why Istvan Hont has with reason maintained that in Hobbes' philosophy there is no place for the economic organisation as cause of state formation. But it also shows the limitation of that interpretation. Perhaps prompted by his desire to write *Leviathan* as handbook for princes, Hobbes does come to realise the need to discuss the material conditions of a flourishing state. But due to the pervasive metaphor that structures those reflections, he does not appropriately integrate these discussions into his scientific system. That is why he fails to tie the premises of his political philosophy, premises that share affinity with those thinkers in the late nineteenth century like Jevons and Edgeworth that formalise economic analysis, to his recommendations to the sovereign with regard to the economic institutions that would ensure the safety and prosperity of the people.

Bibliography

Appleby, Joyce Oldham. 1978. *Economic Thought and Ideology in Seventeenth-Century England.* Princeton: Princeton University Press.

Fleischacker, Samuel. 2004. *On Adam Smith's Wealth of Nations*. Princeton: Princeton University Press.

Force, Pierre. 2003. *Self-Interest Before Adam Smith: A Genealogy of Economic Science.* Cambridge: Cambridge University Press.

Hirschmann, Albert O. 1977. *The Passions and the Interests.* Princeton: Princeton University Press.

Hobbes, Thomas. 1969. *The Elements of Law*, ed. Ferdinand Tönnies. London: Frank Cass & Co, second Edition with a new introduction by M M Goldsmith.

———. 1998. In *On the Citizen*, ed. Richard Tuck and Michael Silverthorne. Cambridge: Cambridge University Press.

———. 2012. In *Leviathan*, ed. Noel Malcolm. Oxford: Oxford University Press.

Hont, Istvan. 2010. *Jealousy of Trade*. Cambridge: Harvard University Press.

Kavka, Gregory S. 1986. *Hobbesian Moral and Political Theory, Studies in Moral, Political, and Legal Philosophy*. Princeton/Guildford: Princeton University Press.

Langholm, Odd. 1998. *The Legacy of Scholasticism in Economic Thought: Antecedents of Choice and Power*. Cambridge: Cambridge University Press.

Levy, Aaron. 1954. Economic Views of Thomas Hobbes. *Journal of the History of Ideas* 15(4): 589–595.
Lukes, Steven. 1968. Methodological Individualism Reconsidered. *The British Journal of Sociology* 19(2): 119–129.
Macpherson, C.B. 1962. *The Political Theory of Possessive Individualism*. Oxford: Clarendon Press.
Malcolm, Noel. 2012. General Introduction. In *Leviathan*, ed. Thomas Hobbes and Noel Malcolm. Oxford: Oxford University Press.
McArthur, Neil. 2012. "Trown Amongst Many": Hobbes on Taxation and Fiscal Policy. In *Hobbes Today*, ed. S.A. Lloyd. Cambridge: Cambridge University Press.
Smith, Adam. 1976. In *An Inquiry into the Nature and Causes of the Wealth of Nations*, ed. R.H. Campbell, A.S. Skinner, and W.B. Todd. Oxford: Oxford University Press.
Taylor, A.E. 1908. *Thomas Hobbes*. London: Archibald Constable.
Taylor, Quentin. 2010. Thomas Hobbes, Political Economist. *The Independent Review* 14(3): 415–433.
Udehn, Lars. 2001. *Methodological Individualism: Background, History and Meaning*. London: Routledge.

Chapter 4
Circulation of Blood and Money in *Leviathan* – Hobbes on the Economy of the Body

Christoffer Basse Eriksen

4.1 Introduction: The Mint of the Body and the Heart of the State

When turning towards the subject of the organic structure of the heart and blood, the physician and natural philosopher Walter Charleton (1619–1707) in his *Three Anatomic Lectures* (1683), reasons that to be able to grasp "this Master-piece of Nature the heart," one should compare it to the "*Hydraulic Machines,*" the best example being the famous mint at Segovia (Charleton 1683, 71).[1] For Charleton, the heart is an automaton working perpetually by means of cardiac heat just as the mint works perpetually by means of the pressure of water. But not only do they share the same form and function, they also serve an analogical *end*, namely "to Coin mony, which is the bloud of all States." Just as the mint transforms ingots of silver and gold into coins and stamps them with the image of the King, the heart stamps "the character of Vitality upon the mass of bloud, for the maintenance of life in all parts of the body, and regulation of the whole Animal œconomy" (Charleton 1683, 72). Although Charleton does make some reservations concerning the analogy, as he sees the heart as a more perfect machine than the mint, the underlying framework is quite clear: The body is a state, the heart is a machine and blood is money. To encounter a money-stamping mint in an anatomical description of the human body might seem a bit strange to a modern reader. For how did it get there? And how come that it enters so seamlessly into the physician Charleton's lecture and thus, we must infer, into his comprehension of the functions of the human body?

---

[1]Charleton lifted this analogy directly from Sir Kenelm Digby, who had witnessed the mint at Segovia at work, cf. Sawday (1983, 28–33; 1995, 242–244) and Thomson (2008, 46).

C.B. Eriksen (✉)
Department of Philosophy and History of Ideas, Aarhus University, Aarhus, Denmark
e-mail: cbe@cas.au.dk

J. Bek-Thomsen et al. (eds.), *History of Economic Rationalities*, Ethical Economy 54, DOI 10.1007/978-3-319-52815-1_4

In the scholarship, the importance of this metaphorology of the body-machine for developments in seventeenth century natural philosophy and especially the life sciences has been examined in detail to the degree that René Descartes' (1596–1650) statement in *L'Homme* (1637) that the body is "just a statue or machine of earth" (Descartes 1998, 99) and its numerous seventeenth century variations is one of the best documented moments in the history of ideas.[2] Less attention, though, has been given to the fact that these mechanical metaphors not only worked to render the living body intelligible, but that a sophisticated discursive interplay emerged knitting the three entities body, machine and state together. Thus such an amphibious being as Charleton's mint, which literally served the economico-governmental function of stamping money and metaphorically the vital function of pumping blood, could appear. And the political theorist and natural philosopher Thomas Hobbes (1588–1679) could argue that the state was "an artificial man" (Hobbes 1996, 7), a living being constructed by living, human beings and working like a living, human being.

In this chapter, I argue that the fact that Hobbes models his state not just on a body or a machine, but on a *living body-machine*, has wide implications for the way that this state is imagined to function. First, I establish that Hobbes in the *Leviathan* (1651) understood the body along the lines of his contemporary William Harvey (1578–1657) who in his 1628 work *Exercitatio Anatomica de Motu Cordis et Sanguinis in Animalibus* (*An Anatomical Exercise on the Motion of the Heart and Blood in Animals*) had established the circulation of the blood as a fundamental principle of the living body. Importantly, Harvey applied mechanical metaphors in his description of the body, but he did not commit himself to a truly mechanist understanding of the body's functions and stayed within an Aristotelian understanding of the organs performing certain functions in the body. This had the implication that when Hobbes extended the Harveian model of the body and especially the emphasis on the circulation of blood to explain certain political functions of the state, he adopted related notions of health and disease which he saw as the effects of a lack of circulation of money. For Hobbes, a sick body is equivalent to a body at war with itself and thus the purpose of the circulatory economy is the prevention of civil war. By emphasizing the degree to which Hobbes' state was an *embodied state*, that is a state modeled on the human body being cut up on the dissection table and studied by physicians, I also make a general case for the impact of the life sciences, medicine and physiology on the development of seventeenth century political philosophy and the corresponding economic rationalities.[3]

[2] For analyses of the body-machine metaphor in early modern natural philosophy, see Duchesneau (1998), Des Chene (2001), Shapiro (2003) and Smith (2011). For the reception of *L'Homme*, see the essays collected in Antoine-Mahut and Gaukroger (2016).

[3] For the discursive role played by the concept of circulation in economic and political thought of seventeenth century England, see Johnson (1966), Finkelstein (2000), Desmedt (2005), Glaisyer (2005), Hont (2005) and Wennerlind (2011). Mirowski (1994), Riskin (2003), and Schabas (2005) make strong cases for the interdependency of economic and natural-philosophical thought in the early modern period.

4.2 The Living Body of the Leviathan

It is somewhat ironic that Thomas Hobbes would be the one to shape one of the greatest metaphors of seventeenth century political thought, the Leviathan, since, in a paragraph concerning the use of metaphors in "all rigorous search of truth", Hobbes writes that "metaphors, they are in this case utterly excluded. For seeing they openly profess deceit; to admit them into counsel, or reasoning, were manifest folly" (Hobbes 1996, 46–47). And yet, how are we to understand the notion of the Leviathan if not as a metaphor?[4]

In the introduction to *Leviathan*, we learn that "by art is created that great LEVIATHAN called a COMMONWEALTH, or STATE, (in Latin CIVITAS) which is but an artificial man" (Hobbes 1996, 7). For Hobbes, the state is made *by* man and *of* man and thus in order to grasp the nature of the state Hobbes considers both "the *matter* hereof, and the *artificer*; both which is *Man*" (Hobbes 1996, 7). So to understand how the state works, according to Hobbes, one must understand how the human body works. For Hobbes, the description of the state as a political *body* is not just a neutral description as when a modern-day philosopher teaching in the classroom uses, say, a piece of chalk, a cup of coffee or a computer as an example of the philosophical distinctions that he or she is making. Rather, the medical body works as a "theory constitutive metaphor", that is a metaphor which does not just didactically explain an already given theory but which instead shapes the theory to such a degree that without this metaphor it would be devoid of content (Boyd 1979, 360; Sawday 1983, 21–22).

In the first chapter of *Leviathan*, "Of Sense", Hobbes employs the empiricist *credo* of "nihil est in intellectu quod non fuerit in sensu" which in Hobbes' version goes: "there is no conception in a man's mind, which hath not at first, totally, or by parts, been begotten upon the organs of sense" (Hobbes 1996, 9). From this, and from natural-philosophical axioms such as "[w]hen a body is once in motion, it moveth (unless something else hinder it) eternally" (*Ibid.*, 11), Hobbes begins step by step to develop the ways in which the interiority of man functions, including the role of speech, reason, the passions, knowledge, manners and religion. Central to this manoeuvre is Hobbes' mechanical-philosophical understanding of matter as inert, his *physics*, but just as important are Hobbes' reflections on the ways in which organized bodies work internally and the natural philosophy that he latches on to here is not mechanics, but medicine. For Hobbes, the correct description of the "organs of sense" and the rest of the organs of the human body is just as important as a correct description of inert bodies in mechanical motion. And while Hobbes draws on the Galilean and Cartesian natural philosophy of his day for his philosophy of corpuscles, he draws on state-of-the-art medical science for his knowledge on sensible bodies. In fact, according to his contemporary biographer John Aubrey

[4] For Hobbes' use of a monster in his description of the state, see Stillman (1995). For the shifting epistemic roles played by monsters in the early modern period, see Daston and Park (1981, 1998, ch. 5).

he was himself part of the medical-scientific *milieu* around the Royal College of Physicians (Aubrey 1898, 336–337; Skinner 1969).

In the prefatory Epistle to *De Corpore* from 1655, Hobbes gives praise to the advancements of the natural philosophy of his day and especially the "science of human bodies" advanced "in special by the wit and industry of physicians, the only true natural philosophers, especially of our most learned men of the College of Physicians in London" (Hobbes 1839, ix). In particular, Hobbes speaks about the physician William Harvey with the following praise:

> Lastly, the science of *man's body*, the most profitable part of natural science, was first discovered with admirable sagacity by our countryman Doctor Harvey, principal Physician to King James and King Charles, in his books of the *Motion of the Blood*, and of the *Generation of Living Creatures*; who is the only man I know, that conquering envy, hath established a new doctrine in his life-time (Hobbes 1839, viii).

Hobbes is referring to Harvey's 1628 work *De Motu Cordis* in which Harvey had established the circulation of blood and the *Exercitationes de generatione animalium* (*Anatomical Exercises on the Generation of Animals*) from 1651 in which Harvey put forth his epigenesist theory of generation (French 1994). Harvey, too, is fond of metaphors. In *De Motu Cordis*' opening dedication to Charles I, he writes of the heart of animals that it "is the foundation of their life, the sovereign of everything within them, the sun of their microcosm" just as the king "is the foundation of his kingdom, the sun of the world around him, the heart of the republic" (Harvey 1847a, 3). Harvey also describes the heart as "a piece of machinery" (Harvey 1847a, 31) which has the function to push the blood around the body through a system of arteries and veins. Harvey showed how this "one-way" circulation worked through observations of the veins and arteries, numerous vivisections of animals and by quantitative measurements of the amount of blood in the body relative to the amount of blood being pumped out by the heart (Harvey 1847a, 45–47; Salter and Wolfe 2009). Following these observations, he noted that the blood wasn't constantly produced, but that it held a constant level and was enlivened in the circulatory system by the heart which, as stated, Harvey believed worked like a pump. By arguing that the veins and arteries made up one connected system, Harvey also denied the existence of certain "drawing forces" of the blood, as imagined by Galenic physicians.

But as recently shown by Peter Distelzweig (2016), we should not take Harvey's use of mechanical metaphors as evidence for him being a mechanist like Descartes, Pierre Gassendi or Robert Boyle. For Harvey, the goal of anatomy was to understand the action, use and function of the parts of the body considered as a whole and thus anatomy aspired to gain true knowledge of the causes of the body (Cunningham 2003; Lennox 2006). Whereas for a mechanist like Descartes, parts should be studied for themselves and not in relation to a whole and no other causes than the efficient cause should be taken into account, a teleological anatomist like Harvey contends that the "that for the sake of which," the end or purpose, of an organ is also a part of the anatomists' field of knowledge.[5] Thus the heart for

[5]Although the range and purity of Descartes' mechanism when it comes to living bodies, especially, is a pressing point in recent scholarship on Descartes. See (Hutchins et al. 2016) for an overview of these debates.

Harvey is not intelligible in itself, but must be studied and understood as part of a larger system, namely that of the circulation of blood. When Harvey in *De Motu Cordis* and *De generatione animalium* looks for the moment when life emerges in developing chicks or the moment when life fades away from the animals that he is vivisecting, it is the pulse which is the crucial point, not the organ of the heart in itself (Harvey 1847a, 27, c, 374). For Harvey, a lack of circulation of blood in the animal is a sign of lack of life (Bertoloni Meli 2016, 104–112).

Harvey's teleological understanding of the body is overtly in conflict with Hobbes' alleged mechanism, a point which raises curiosity about Hobbes' praise of Harvey. Here, I will not attempt to resolve this conflict, but instead examine the consequences that follow from the fact that Hobbes models his view on the circulation of money in the state on Harvey's description of the circulation of blood in the body.

4.3 The Economy of the Leviathan

Hobbes only mentions the word "economy" once in *Leviathan*, namely in the chapter "Of the Public Ministers of Sovereign Power", which discusses the "hands" of the commonwealth, or the ministers of different kinds: commanding soldiers, teachers, judges and ambassadors. The public ministers dealing with the "economy of a commonwealth" are those taking care of the treasure, tax collection and public revenue, although how this takes place and how the treasure is to be cultivated is not commented on by Hobbes (Hobbes 1996, 160). Thus, economic affairs are a matter for the state but on a par with issues regarding the military and judicial system and as such a part of the maintenance of the commonwealth in general, not as a special part and indeed not as something which is extraneous to the sovereign's affairs.

This view is underlined in the following chapter which deals more extensively with issues of economic life. In the chapter called "Of the Nutrition, and Procreation of a Commonwealth" the body metaphor plays a central role as Hobbes here describes how the commonwealth stays nourished, healthy and alive. The key concepts are here *propriety*, the fact that subjects in a commonwealth are able to have and maintain private property, and *distribution*, the way in which movable property is exchanged. Interestingly, the two concepts are interdependent meaning that you cannot, according to Hobbes, have private property without a proper distribution and, likewise, you cannot have distribution without private property, or, in Hobbes' words: "The distribution of the materials of this nourishment, is the constitution of *mine*, and *thine*, and *his*; that is to say, in one word *propriety*" (Hobbes 1996, 164).

Considered this way, economy, or the distribution of nourishment, plays a very significant role in the establishment and existence of the commonwealth seeing that if there were no distribution then (1) subjects of the commonwealth would not be subjects capable of propriety and (2) the commonwealth would not be nourished which ultimately would imply its death. In these passages, the *organic scheme* under which Hobbes considers the state becomes very clear. Central is the interdependence or balance of the parts of the body not unlike what Charleton calls animal economy that is as signifying an *order* of a system. In this system, the fluids of the body are not flowing freely but are regulated in a predefined structure which they in turn are rendering capable of continuous existence as they give life to the centers of the circulatory system (Wolfe and Terada 2008, 546; Balan 1975, 289).

In the chapter on the nutrition and procreation of the commonwealth, Hobbes has a passage on "The conduits and way of money to the public use" (Hobbes 1996, 168). On the subject of the circulation of money in the commonwealth, Hobbes writes: "And in this also, the artificial man maintains his resemblance with the natural; whose veins receiving the blood from the several parts of the body, carry it to the heart; where being made vital, the heart by the arteries sends it out again, to enliven, and enable for motion all the members of the same" (Hobbes 1996, 168). Several things are interesting in the passage. First of all, Hobbes' very technical description is striking: Hobbes explains how the blood is received in the outer parts of the body, transported through the veins back to the heart and then pushed out through the arteries into the body parts again. The novelty of Harvey's discovery in *De Motu Cordis* had, as described above, been to determine the connection between the arterial and venous systems of blood and his argument that these two systems were indeed one where the blood was, as Hobbes rightly describes it, pushed from the heart through the arteries and back through the veins.

Hobbes' description makes it clear that he is referring to "Harvey's body," but the question is which implications for Hobbes' theory this has. To distinguish this, let's look closer at Hobbes' comments on the members of the body. Hobbes emphasizes that the blood enlivens and enables for motion all the members of the political body. A member, it must be remembered, signifies both a body part and a subject of a community. Thus, Hobbes' idea seems to be that just like a body member, say, a toe or an arm, cut off from the circulatory network of blood withers away and ultimately dies, a subject excluded from the circulation of money dies in the sense that it becomes excluded from the commonwealth. But this also functions in a positive sense as the circulation of money enables outer members of the political body to be *incorporated* into the commonwealth. As they become integrated into the circulation they are 'born' as members of the commonwealth and as long as they stay inside the circulatory system, they continue to be so.

This should be understood in extension of Hobbes' comments on *propriety* earlier on in the chapter. Here, Hobbes argues that in a territory without a covenant and sovereign power, who, it must be remembered, is the "artificial *soul*" of the body (Hobbes 1996, 7), there would be no propriety at all as everything would be owned only by those who "getteth it, and keepeth it by force" (Hobbes 1996, 164). This is the image of a body at war with itself as the members instead of working together would seek to kill each other and deprive each other of their riches. Thus, seeing that there would be no sovereign power to ensure the legitimacy of properties and the distribution thereof there would be "neither *propriety*, nor *community*; but *uncertainty*" (ibid.).

For Hobbes, the parts cannot live without being incorporated into the system of circulation but neither can the whole live without having a proper circulation between the parts. Having subjects who inhabit a degree of relative autonomy being able to own property and trade this property enables the sovereign to extend his power throughout the whole political body. Seeing that it is the sovereign that is the ultimate arbiter of all transactions, these transactions expand his power although they are not directly being made by the sovereign. Hobbes explains this in the following way:

> And therefore it belongeth to the commonwealth, (that is to say, to the sovereign,) to appoint in what manner, all kinds of contract between subjects, (as buying, selling, exchanging, borrowing, lending, letting, and taking to hire,) are to be made; and by what words and signs they shall be understood for valid. And for the matter, and distribution of the nourishment, to the several members of the commonwealth, thus much (considering the model of the whole work) is sufficient (Hobbes 1996, 167).

Nourishment is here the key term. As the commonwealth is envisioned as a living body, it has to be nourished just like any living body. And the nourishment, it is here implied, is the trade itself. Hobbes makes this explicit in the following passage:

> By the means of which measures, all commodities, movable and immovable, are made to accompany a man to all places of his resort, within and without the place of his ordinary residence; and the same passeth from man to man, within the commonwealth; and goes round about, nourishing (as it passeth) every part thereof; in so much as this concoction, is as it were the sanguification of the commonwealth: for natural blood is in like manner made of the fruits of the earth; and circulating, nourisheth by the way every member of the body of man (Hobbes 1996, 167).

This sanguification of the political body is important as it emphasizes to which extent Hobbes' state is an *embodied state*. While the sovereign may be the most important character in the state, "the soul of the body," he couldn't exist and couldn't be sovereign had he not a body and all the body parts to rule over; the sovereign needs all the semi-autonomous subjects in able to exist at all. So had the political body no pulse, no circulation, it would not be able to exist at all. This quality is a direct consequence of the weight that Hobbes gives to the circulation of money and as such it is a direct consequence of his usage of the Harveian framework.

4.4 Health, Balance and Civil War

The idea that a lack of circulation may cause the death of the body is already, though in a subtle way, mentioned in the introduction to *Leviathan*. In his list of analogies between the body natural and the body politic, Hobbes concludes by drawing up the following analogies: "*concord*, *health*; *sedition*, *sickness*; and *civil war*, *death*" (Hobbes 1996, 7). From this list we learn that the political body is healthy when the members are in concordance, ill when people have a tendency to mutiny or rebellion and, lastly, that the political body is dead when in a state of civil war. Civil war is thus the worst condition that a commonwealth can be in, or, more correctly, it is the state in which there isn't any commonwealth any longer: The state of nature.

In the chapter "Of Those Things that Weaken, or Tend to the Dissolution of a Commonwealth," Hobbes extrapolates on this analogy and explains the different threats to a commonwealth as different *diseases*. Rebellions who are disputing against the sovereign cause *intestinal damage* and are "like the little worms, which physicians call *ascarides*" (Hobbes 1996, 221), a commonwealth with a mixed government is compared to the monstrous state of "a man, that had another man growing out of his side" (Hobbes 1996, 219) and, most interestingly, Hobbes describes "a disease, which resembleth the pleurisy" which is when "the treasure of the commonwealth, flowing out of its due course, is gathered together in too much abundance, in one, or a few private men, by monopolies or by farms of the public revenues; in the same manner as the blood in a pleurisy, getting into the membrane of the breast, breedeth there an inflammation, accompanied with a fever, and painful stitches" (Hobbes 1996, 220). The Leviathan, of course, is a monster, but it is a monster capable of being healthy and thus the body of this monster is normal in a medical sense. On the contrary, these examples are highlighting pathological political bodies which are not capable to maintain their lives.

This pathology in the economy of the political body is caused by people or corporations not *doing what they're supposed to do*, that is hoarding too much money and thus causing a lack of money elsewhere. The circulation of money is here, as was typical for the mercantile tradition, seen as a zero-sum game just as Harvey had shown that the circulation of blood is a zero-sum game and that there is a fixed volume of blood in the body (Finkelstein 2000, 89–97). Another way to phrase this, and one closer to the vocabulary of both Hobbes and Harvey, is to say that "farms of the public revenues" gathering too much money are not "performing [their] work" properly (Harvey 1847a: 32). The concepts *motu*, *action* and *functio*, or *motion*, *action* and *office* are used regularly by Harvey for example in the chapter heading "Of the motion, action, and office of the heart" (Harvey 1847a: 31) from *De Motu Cordis* or when, in the "First Disquisition to John Riolan" from 1649, Harvey speaks about "the end and office of all veins being to receive the blood brought by the arteries" (Harvey 1847b: 100). One of the best examples of this vocabulary is found in *De generatione animalium* where Harvey in a phrase very similar to Hobbes' comment on the pleurisy writes that the liver cannot "perform its office without the influence of the blood (…); nor does it perform any duty until it is penetrated with blood" (Harvey 1847c: 437–438). Hobbes, discussing the offices of sovereign representatives, writes that a "commander of an army in chief, if he be not popular, shall not be beloved, nor feared as he ought to be by his army; and consequently, cannot perform that office with good success" (Hobbes 1996: 234).

Central to these remarks is a sense of *balance* and *harmony* of the body. In order for there to be a due course of the blood the different officers or organs need to do their part without claiming too much money, power or blood so that a proper circulation can be upheld. The purposes of these offices are, then, both the offices themselves but also the work of the offices in relation to the balance of the whole, which is to say the health of the body. Likewise, just as the circulation of blood is central for the maintenance of the health of the natural body for Harvey, the circulation of money, the *economy*, is, for Hobbes, not something extraneous to the political body but in a literal sense internal to it and necessary for its existence.

4.5 Conclusion

Hobbes is not the only one to have described the economy of a political entity as a circulation of fluids. In eighteenth century France, we find the blood-money metaphor applied by economic thinkers such as Rousseau and the Physiocrats, although here the tone of the metaphor shifted towards an interest in maintaining equilibrium between opposing states, something absent in Hobbesian thought, just as the newly discovered "electrical fire" eventually became the element superseding blood in the metaphor (Rousseau 1997, 6; Turgot 1973, 158; Christensen 1994; Riskin 2002, 105–137; 2003). That the metaphor was used widely and through a long period of time only forces us to pay more attention to the specific ways that it was used in specific texts and contexts.

For Hobbes, the linkage between circulating money and circulating blood was important as he needed a firm and secure science on which to model something as complex as the mechanisms of the state. Harvey's theory of the circulation of blood stood out for him as a prime example of state-of-the-art Royal science, and thus this theory provided him with the institutional and epistemological solidity he needed after having refused the *scientiae* of the still prevalent School philosophy. But Harvey's theory was not free of its own implications and preconceptions, and his view of the body as a system of functional parts conveyed Hobbes' political body with an emphasis on the constant, regulated flux of nourishment. This implied a preoccupation with the borders of the political body and with securing the cohesion of everything within these borders.

Hobbes emphasizes that his Leviathan is to be understood as a "*Mortal God*" (Hobbes 1996, 114) which means that the commonwealth is not eternal and that it can be disbanded. In other words, the state, like man and unlike God, has a life expectancy, can succumb to diseases and ultimately die. The circulation of money, the economy, should be viewed in this light. As I have argued, Hobbes imagines that an improper circulation will lead to diseases while a proper circulation will preserve the strength of the political body. Hobbes did not regard the economic sphere as distinct from the political sphere, but as vital a part as life is to the living body.

Bibliography

Antoine-Mahut, Delphine, and Stephen Gaukroger. 2016. *Descartes' Treatise on Man and Its Reception*. Dordrecht: Springer.

Aubrey, John. 1898. *Brief Lives Chiefly of Contemporaries Set Down by John Aubrey, Between the Years 1669 & 1696*. Vol. 1. Oxford: Clarendon Press.

Balan, Bernard. 1975. Premières recherches sur l'origine et la formation du concept d'économie animale. *Revue d'histoire des sciences* 28: 289–326.

Bertoloni Meli, Domenico. 2016. Machines of the Body in the Seventeenth Century. In *Early Modern Medicine and Natural Philosophy*, ed. Peter Distelzweig et al., 91–116. Dordrecht: Springer.

Boyd, Richard. 1979. Metaphor and Theory Change: What is a 'Metaphor' a Metaphor For? In *Metaphor and Thought*, ed. Andrew Ortony. Cambridge: Cambridge University Press.

Charleton, Walter. 1683. *Three Anatomic Lectures*. London: Walter Kettilby.

Christensen, P. 1994. Fire, Motion, and Productivity: The Proto-Energetics of Nature and Economy in François Quesnay. In *Natural Images in Economic Thought: "Markets Read in Tooth and Claw"*, ed. Philip Mirowski, 249–288. Cambridge: Cambridge University Press.

Cunningham, Andrew. 2003. The Pen and the Sword: Recovering the Disciplinary Identity of Physiology and Anatomy Before 1800 II: Old Anatomy – The Sword. *Studies in History and Philosophy of Biological and Biomedical Sciences* 34: 51–76.

Daston, Lorraine, and Katherine Park. 1981. Unnatural Conceptions: The Study of Monsters in Sixteenth- and Seventeenth-Century France and England. *Past and Present* 92: 20–54.

Daston, Lorraine; Park, Katherine. 1998. *Wonders and the Order of Nature, 1150–1750*. New York: Zone Books.

Des Chene, Dennis. 2001. *Spirits and Clock: Machine and Organism in Descartes*. Ithaca: Cornell University Press.

Descartes, René. 1998. *The World and Other Writings*. Trans. and ed. Stephen Gaukroger. Cambridge: Cambridge University Press.

Desmedt, Ludovic. 2005. Money in the 'Body Politick': The Analysis of Trade and Circulation in the Writings of Seventeenth-Century Political Arithmeticians. *History of Political Economy* 37(1): 79–101.

Distelzweig, Peter. 2016. "Mechanics" and Mechanism in William Harvey's Anatomy: Varieties and Limits. In *Early Modern Medicine and Natural Philosophy*, ed. Peter Distelzweig et al., 117–140. Dordrecht: Springer.

Duchesneau, François. 1998. *Les modèles du vivant de Descartes à Leibniz*. Paris: Vrin.

Finkelstein, Andrea. 2000. *Harmony and the Balance*. Michigan: The University of Michigan Press.

French, Roger. 1994. *William Harvey's Natural Philosophy*. Cambridge: Cambridge University Press.

Glaisyer, Natasha. 2005. 'A Due Circulation in the Veins of the Publick': Imagining Credit in Late Seventeenth- and Early Eighteenth-Century England. *The Eighteenth Century* 46(3): 277–297.

Harvey, William. 1847a. An Anatomical Disquisition on the Motion of Heart and Blood in Animals. In *The Works of William Harvey, M. D*, ed. Robert Willis. London: The Sydenham Society.

———. 1847b. An Anatomical Disquisition on the Circulation of the Blood to John Riolan. In *The Works of William Harvey, M. D*, ed. Robert Willis. London: The Sydenham Society.

———. 1847c. On the Generation of Animals. In *The Works of William Harvey, M. D*, ed. Robert Willis. London: The Sydenham Society.

Hobbes, Thomas. 1839. *The English Works of Thomas Hobbes of Malmesbury*. London: John Bohn.

———. 1996. *Leviathan*. Oxford: Oxford University Press.

Hont, Istvan. 2005. *Jealousy of Trade*. Cambridge: Harvard University Press.

Hutchins, Barnaby, Christoffer Basse Eriksen and Charles T. Wolfe. 2016. The Embodied Descartes: Contemporary Readings of L'Homme. In *Descartes' Treatise on Man and Its Reception*, ed. Delphine Antoine-Mahut and Stephen Gaukroger, 287–304. Dordrecht: Springer.

Johnson, Jerah. 1966. The Money = Blood Metaphor, 1300–1800. *The Journal of Finance* 21: 119–122.

Lennox, James G. 2006. The Comparative Study of Animal Development: William Harvey's Aristotelianism. In *The Problem of Animal Generation in Early Modern Philosophy*, ed. Justin E.H. Smith, 21–46. Cambridge: Cambridge University Press.

Mirowski, Philip, ed. 1994. *Natural Images in Economic Thought: "Markets Read in Tooth and Claw"*. Cambridge: Cambridge University Press.

Riskin, Jessica. 2002. *Science in the Age of Sensibility*. Chicago: Chicago University Press.

———. 2003. The "Spirit of Systems" and the Fortunes of Physiocracy. *History of Political Economy* 35: 42–73.

Rousseau, Jean-Jacques. 1997. Discourse of Political Economy. In *The Social Contract and Other Later Political Writings, Rousseau, Jean-Jacques*. Cambridge: Cambridge University Press.

Salter, Alan, and Charles T. Wolfe. 2009. Empiricism contra Experiment: Harvey, Locke and the Revisionist View of Experimental Philosophy. *Bulletin d'Histoire et d'Épistémologie des sciences de la vie* 16(2): 113–140.

Sawday, Jonathan. 1983. The Mint at Segovia: Digby, Hobbes, Charleton, and the Body as a Machine in the Seventeenth Century. *Prose Studies: History, Theory, Criticism* 6: 21–35.

———. 1995. *The Body Emblazoned: Dissection and the Human Body in Renaissance Culture*. London: Routledge.

Schabas, Margaret. 2005. *The Natural Origins of Economics*. Chicago: The University of Chicago Press.

Shapiro, Lisa. 2003. The Health of the Body-Machine? or, Seventeenth Century Mechanism and the Concept of Health. *Perspectives on Science* 11(4): 421–442.

Skinner, Quentin. 1969. Thomas Hobbes and the Nature of the Early Royal Society. *The Historical Journal* 12(2): 217–239.

Smith, Justin E.H. 2011. *Divine Machines: Leibniz and the Sciences of Life*. Princeton: Princeton University Press.

Stillman, Robert E. 1995. Hobbes' "Leviathan": Monsters, Metaphors, and Magic. *ELH* 62(4): 791–819.

Thomson, Ann. 2008. *Bodies of Thought: Science, Religion, and the Soul in the Early Enlightenment*. Oxford: Oxford University Press.

Turgot, Anne-Robert-Jacques. 1973. Reflections of the Formation and Distribution of Wealth. In *Turgot on Progress, Sociology and Economics*, ed. Ronald M. Meek. Cambridge: Cambridge University Press.

Wennerlind, Carl. 2011. *Casualties of Credit: The English Financial Revolution, 1620–1720*. Cambridge: Harvard University Press.

Wolfe, Charles T., and Motoichi Terada. 2008. The Animal Economy as Object and Program in Montpellier Vitalism. *Science in Context* 21(4): 537–579.

Chapter 5
Profits and Morals in Leon Battista Alberti's *I libri della famiglia*

Jakob Bek-Thomsen

There is something intrinsically fascinating about growth and its presence in contemporary society. In today's media and public debate, the concept of growth has become shorthand for *economic growth* and is presented as both a measure of success and a necessary means for progress. One might go as far as to say that growth is a fundamental concept of modern civilization. Politicians and economists use growth continuously to estimate the well being of a state, a business or even the entire world summed up in GNPs or revenues. As such, economic growth has immense power and jurisdiction as an identifier of valued or non-valued societal actions and practices. It has been the driving force of economics since its emergence as a scientific discipline (Aghion and Durlauf 2005, xi). Having growth as a *sine qua non* concept of economics means it influences all other aspects of the economic. For instance, wealth is *created* through production, and this increase is understood to be unlimited or endless:

> Is it true, as is sometimes alleged, that exponential growth in the economy will eventually use up the fixed stock of resources? Well yes, it is true in the limited sense that current theories suggest the universe will one day run down. However, this seems more of a concern for a course in astrophysics, or perhaps theology, than for a course in economics. Over any interesting horizon, the economy is protected from resource-depletion disasters by two factors. First, technical progress permits us to produce more using fewer resources. For example, the energy efficiency of room lighting has increased by a factor of 4500 since Neolithic times. Second, as specific resources come into short supply, their prices rise, leading producers to shift toward substitutes. (Dornbusch et al. 2011, 90)

However, economic textbooks will often explain how earlier conceptions of economic growth bear no resemblance to a modern definition of it and will insist that the classical theories are best labeled *development* theories rather than growth theories (Shearer 1961; Sandmo 2011; Mokyr 2007). Within these lines we have a range

J. Bek-Thomsen (✉)
Institute for Culture and Society, Aarhus University, Aarhus, Denmark
e-mail: idejbt@cas.au.dk

J. Bek-Thomsen et al. (eds.), *History of Economic Rationalities*, Ethical Economy 54, DOI 10.1007/978-3-319-52815-1_5

of literature, perhaps still dominated by the works of J.B. Bury and Robert Nisbit on the history of the ideas of progress that considers both biological and social aspects of the concept (Nisbet 1994; Bury 1987). However, at the most basic level classical theories as well as modern economics are built on a linear, seemingly limitless perspective of time and history.

In the present chapter, I want to take a look at the early intellectual history of growth – more specifically the history of the concept before the birth of political economy and try to grasp at certain fundamental traits associated with different ideas about growth. I've chosen to focus on Leon Battista Alberti's two distinctive economic ideas – his *motives* for seeking profit and his manual for *obtaining* profit. The ideas I'm looking at are NOT about economic growth. They are about growth in different forms and shapes – which existed before the birth of political economy. They represent other ways of thinking about and acting with economic issues. In effect they become economic rationalities.

***

> Riches however, are for nearly everyone the primary reason for working at all. They are also most useful in making it possible to persevere in our undertakings until we win approval and attain public favor, position, and fame. This is the time, therefore, to explain how wealth is acquired and how it is kept. It was also one of the four things which we said were necessary to bring about and to preserve contentment in a family. Now then let us begin to accumulate wealth. (Alberti 1969, 141)

With such a seemingly harmless paragraph, the humanist artist Leon Battista Alberti (1404–1472) created ammunition for one of the most ensuing debates of the sociological and economic sciences in the twentieth century. Following Max Weber's *The Protestant Ethic and the Spirit of Capitalism* ([1904/1905] 1930) this battle concerning the origins of modern capitalism was fought in Werner Sombart's *The Quintessence of Capitalism* ([1913] 1915), which sought to undermine Weber's thesis of the Calvinist importance to capitalism by reference to Alberti's *I libri della famiglia*. Weber responded to Sombart's criticism in the second edition of this book wherein he dismissed Alberti as identical to his own capitalist figure of Benjamin Franklin. Much have been said about origins, truths, misinterpretations and omissions in the quarrel of the capitalist spirit and this is not the place to advance any deeper analysis of this discussion. Following Jan Rehmann, I want to emphasize one aspect of the debate which deals with the question of whether Alberti's virtuous (avoiding ethical) behavior is religious in origin (Rehmann 2011, 370–373). The pending question is from where Alberti's justification of activities such as buying, selling, lending and claiming money came from? These activities were solely directed at making a profit that could generate the accumulation of wealth and was thereby of a particular dubious nature (Alberti 1969, 142). Rehmann explains how Alberti "exploits religion" for his ethical justification of the accumulation of wealth. Rather than exploitation, this is a form of economic rationality that borrows its arguments and authorization from the religious. When Alberti speaks of the accumulation of wealth, he does so within specific boundaries intended both to satisfy the

Catholic restraints on economic activities and to ensure that wealth is reinvested in both the family business and the nearby society. In effect, he manages to create an image of the proper economic administration as a visual and economic representation of a good religious life. This is a highly interesting argument and points to the fact that economic ideas during the fifteenth century included reflections on monetary growth.

We will return to Alberti and his book of the family below but before it is necessary to look closer at the ideas of growth and progress, which preceded him, beginning med Hesiod and his poem *Works and Days*[1]:

> Do not put things off till tomorrow and the next day. A man of ineffectual labour, a postpone, does not fill his granary: it is application that promotes your cultivation, whereas a postponer of labour is constantly wrestling with Blights. (Hesiod 1988, 49)

Around 700 BC Hesiod composed his poem of the conditions of human – especially agricultural – life and moral advices on how mankind can live up to his full potential. The historian Frederick Teggart identified *Works and Days* as the first written account of human progress:

> Hesiod set before men the first idea of human progress: the idea that a good life is attainable; that this attainment is dependent upon the thought and activity of men themselves; that the essential requisite is the actuation of the members of the community by a common regard for justice. (Teggart 1947, 77)

Hesiod followed the Greek tradition of looking back to evaluate of the present: to the time when man had lived as a savage beast, but advanced through the acquisition of *cultural principles*, handed down from the deities above. And yet still the present age was a troublesome and evil state. The question for mankind was therefore how one could achieve a desirable life? The answer was through evenhanded justice. A justice which took into account the labour and activities of men and the moral superiority that came with these.

Here, it is important to consider the concepts of time and history in Greek thought. Time was circular but not repetitive. The most obvious example is the passing of each day. Every day follows the same format, but is filled with different inputs. One of the earliest accounts of this is from the Mesopotamian Epic of Gilgamesh, which starts and ends in the same place, with the building of Uruk's wall. Everything has changed for Gilgamesh, yet everything stays the same. The economist Tomas Sedlacek has used the epic to analyze economic thinking within, what he calls "meta-economics": myths, religion, theology, philosophy and science. Despite all the changes Gilgamesh goes through in his quest for immortality he ends up in the city from where he started, still constructing his wall (Sedlacek 2011, 43). A similar conception of time is present in *Works and Days* although it is important to emphasize that Hesiod – or any of the other Greek thinkers – never longed for a return to the past times. It was a matter of improving the present state to something

[1] I follow Robert Nisbet in his advocation that there was indeed ideas of progress in Greek Antiquity and that it is not only a modern idea as argued by J.B. Bury and others. See (Nisbet 1994, 10–13).

better, to progress *through* the cyclical nature of time and history. This might strike us as paradoxical but it was far from it for the ancient Greeks.

There are many examples of ideas of progress in ancient Greek and Roman thought. Nisbet convincingly argues how progress and development were instrumental to philosophers, historians and politicians (Nisbet 1994, 10–46).[2] The reason to highlight Hesiod in this connection is his lowly perspective from a farmer's life with the daily struggles he endures. Through his daily challenges he prescribes a moral vision of how to create a just society with diligence and effort. Armed with these qualities, the individual as well as the collective can grow and progress. Some modern economists are eager to label Hesiod the first economist in history because of his focus on work as the source of wealth and population growth:

> It is from work that men are rich in flocks and wealthy, and a working man is much dearer to the immortals. Work is no reproach, but not working is a reproach; and if you work, it will readily come about that a whorkshy man will envy you as you become wealthy. Wealth brings fortune and prestige. (Hesiod 1988, 46)

This early connection between work and wealth is perhaps banal and obvious. However, it is also a highly interesting argument that wealth is raised to a divine (immortal) property that is to be striven for. Through wealth men can attain fortune and prestige but only when it comes from work. Wealth that is seized forcedly or "shamelessly" will not last. The economic is very closely linked with the individual and personal prosperity. But wealth is also a way of signaling a proper conduct and moral attitude.

***

With the connection between wealth and morals and a direct link between an increase of material goods and proper behavior it is clear to see the heritage from Hesiod and also Xenophon in Alberti's manual for the ideal construction and management of the family. *Oikonomia* – the proper administration of the household – was not merely a concept for maintaining the family at a sustainable level of living. It was also about making a profit and to make those profits grow:

> Profits [guadagno] can grow only as the affairs themselves expand, and with them our industry and labor. Great affairs bring great profits, but in these, as no one doubts, fortune is often vitally involved. (Alberti 1969, 146)

This quote is actually from the end of the second book of the family, which deals with marriage. Here Alberti demonstrates how to maintain a good family relationship before he turns to the more systematic ways of administrating ones economy in

---

[2]The canon of progress in Antiquity which Nisbet studies are: Hesiod, Xenophanes, Aeschylus, Protagoras, Thucydides, Plato and Aristotle. Growth takes different forms and shapes in Greek philosophy. With Aristotle we have the sharp distinction between chremastitics and oikonomia, where the moral authority of the former was strictly dependent on the way in which profit was made. Profit from moneylending, the taking of interest, were not only morally wrong it was also unnatural (Aristotle 1944, 51). Also see (Singer 1958) for an analysis of the Aristotelian concept of oikonomia.

the third book. Two things are important: (1) Alberti argues that it is good when profits grow, and (2) that fortune plays a crucial role in the acquisition of great profits.

This is quite clearly an argument of profit seeking business that even advocates the expansion of business in order to increase the revenue: "From small business affairs no great profits come, however vigorously the enterprise is carried through," Alberti proclaims (Alberti 1969, 146). Taken out of context this could be read as a strangely modern capitalist argument. However, it is obviously far from it. Alberti's advice on how to secure a good family was to invest the profits from small businesses in larger enterprises, which included international import and export. This also increased the risk of loosing the invested profit:

> How many risks they ran, how many rivers and barriers they traversed, before they rested in security! Thieves, tyrants, wars, negligence, cheating on the part of middlemen, all these things did not fail to threaten them. (Alberti 1969, 147)

Fortune – or fate – thus plays a great part to the profit seeking enterprise but those who dares not take the rise of loosing profit to fortune also forfeits the chance to increase the revenue. Those who do however become "leaders in great enterprise, men of the highest usefulness to the country, bringers of honor and fame to the family, men who grow from day to day, not only in money and goods but likewise in dignity and in the eyes of men" (Alberti 1969, 147).

By pointing to the effects of fortune in profitmaking Alberti also highlighted that profit was obtained by different characteristics. One way was through everyone's own individual effort by use of the skills, intellect and physical attributes he or she had been given. Another way was through fortune alone, "finding hidden treasure, inheritance, receiving gifts" but also directly from "things" [cose] which could include usury, wood, agriculture, horse and the like. These "things" bore a profit in themselves without much individual effort or good fortune. It is quite extraordinary that Alberti mentions usury as a source of profit without any form of moral judgment. However, he is stating as a matter of fact that usury *can* bring profit. Not that it should or that he recommends it as a profession. His ambition is to provide a manual for the profitmaking family, which still acts in accordance with a good moral conduct. The outcome of the battle between virtues and vices in every man decided his reputation and social standing which was of far greater importance than material wealth. But the two was intrinsically bound together:

> It is greater profit, truly, to gain favor and praise, since it is for favor and praise that men seek abounding wealth. [...] This is why we do not scorn riches, but learn to govern ourselves and to subdue our desires while we live free and happy in the midst of affluence and abundance. (Alberti 1969, 148)

Freedom was the actual goal of wealth.[3] A freedom of the body and of the spirit so that it was not forced by moral vices such as avarice, timidity and suspiciousness but also other people, was the result of a profitmaking enterprise. Working for others

[3] "Our only use of wealth must be to make us free" (Alberti 1969, 148).

only meant that others would have to share ones profit and thereby limit the possibilities of the workingman to invest his profits in greater businesses.

Having established the motives of profitmaking and the different ways to earn a small or larger profit, Alberti turns to the more systematic account of good management [oikonomia]: "it constitutes half the art of being wealthy" (Alberti 1969, 150). It seems evidently clear that being rich [diventar ricco] was a very strong motive for the use of proper *oikonomia*.

***

The entire third book of the family concerns different aspects of good management: thriftiness and idleness, recordkeeping and task management of employees, and the training of a wife to be a good administrator. For the present purpose of looking at growth it is necessary to focus on the final part of the book where Alberti, through the voice of Giannozo, discussed the advantages and disadvantages of money and property. The two young Alberti family members, who acts as audience and Socratic interlocutors, are unconvinced that land rather than money should be better guarded against Fortune's whims, and that property or crops may just as easily be destroyed as money may be stolen or disappear in a bankruptcy. Giannozo explains:

> The good father knows all his wealth and does not like to see it all in one place or all invested in one thing. If enemies attack or adverse fortune presses you on one side it is good to be strong and have resources on the other. If things are risky here, you save them there. If fortune does not smile on you in one enterprise, it will not strike you in the other too. Therefore, I am not in favor of having only lands or only money. Better have some of this and some of that some stowed far away and located at a variety of places. Moreover, the returns of all should be used for your needs, and the surplus saved for the future. (Alberti 1969, 235)

Alberti stresses the importance of lowering the risk of a loss in revenue by spreading the investment in the household's agricultural production to a range of products. It was not good economy to focus solely on apples or grains, and one should instead produce as many products as possible. This would lower the risk if one crop or product should fail and would also add to the level of self-sustainment that Alberti saw as good economic practice. We can label this Alberti's micromanagement of the household economy. From the last part of the second book on the family we have already seen his advice on "macroeconomic" activities – economic activities that was aimed outside the household and had the purpose of increasing the wealth of the family. The surplus obtained through the proper household administration was thus – if one had the inclination and nerves to handle the increased risks – available to generate an even greater revenue which of course had to be placed evenly in land, production and a monetary reserve.

Profit alone was obviously not a satisfactory legitimation of economic activities during the 1400s. Alberti's book on the family is evidence that any economic rationality had to borrow its legitimacy from somewhere else. In this case it came from religious and philosophic morality. Proper conduct and care in economic affairs were examples of a good moral character who served himself, society and God. On the contrary, carelessness and idleness in economic affairs were the result of a bad – even disrespectful – moral character which could never obtain the praise and acknowledgement from society that was so essential to Renaissance careers (McLean 2007). It is a historic curiosity that the man now known as the one who helped popularize double-entry bookkeeping, Luca Pacioli was at a time a resident of Leon Battista Alberti (Grafton 2000, 197). Pacioli would, many years after his stay with Alberti, publish his *Particularis de Computis et Scripturis* which explained the technical particulars of his bookkeeping method. However, he also explicitly stated that the purpose of bookkeeping was to earn an honest and fair profit because of which every book should begin in the name of God. God was called upon as a witness of the account thereby legitimizing it as an honest and just measurement of economic affairs. By keeping a book, and recording it with diligence and honesty was a way to ensure God's favor and not least the respect of society (Aho 2005, 43–54; Pacioli 1924). Pacioli's thoughts echo Alberti's from 50 years earlier: "In public affairs and in every aspect of civic life, it is a good sign if a merchant has ink-stained fingers" (Alberti 1969, 197). The ink-stained fingers were evidence that the merchant or father of the family led a diligent life and could be trusted on his word. It was the visible extension of his good moral character.

***

The idea of economic growth did not appear until the manifestation of economics as an economic discipline. Among those whom we consider the first of the political economist there is perhaps ideas of progress in connection with the accumulation of capital but it was far from an analysis and comparison of income at distinct periods of time. That came much later. What we find in Alberti is neither a measurement of economic growth but it is definitely an awareness of what an increasing capital holding can do for the individual's possibilities and of how that may help to better ones social standing. Alberti's manual is a very concise example of how Early Modern families were able to circumvent the restrictions on economic activities and redefine them as examples of good moral behavior. Perhaps when we consider economic growth today it is important to remember why we originally thought it as something "good" to acquire and build a fortune.

Bibliography

Aghion, Philippe, and Steven N. Durlauf. 2005. *Handbook of Economic Growth*. 1st ed, *Handbooks in Economics*. Amsterdam: Elsevier.

Aho, James. 2005. *Confession and Bookkeeping: The Religious, Moral, and Rhetorical Roots of Modern Accounting*. Albany: State University of New York Press.

Alberti, Leon Battista. 1969. *The Family in Renaissance Florence*. Trans. R. Watkins. Columbia: University of South Carolina Press.

Aristotle. 1944. *Politics*. Trans. H. Rackham. Cambridge, MA: Harvard University Press.

Bury, J.B. 1987. *The Idea of Progress: An Inquiry Into Its Origin and Growth*. New York: Dover Publications.

Dornbusch, Rudiger, Stanley Fischer, and Richard Startz. 2011. *Macroeconomics*. 11th ed. New York: McGraw-Hill Higher Education.
Grafton, Anthony. 2000. *Leon Battista Alberti: Master Builder of the Italian Renaissance*. 1st ed. New York: Hill and Wang.
Hesiod. 1988. *Theogony and Works and Days*. Trans. M. L. West, *World's Classics*. Oxford Oxfordshire/New York: Oxford University Press.
McLean, Paul D. 2007. *The Art of the Network: Strategic Interaction and Patronage in Renaissance Florence*. Durham: Duke University Press.
Mirowski, Philip. 1989. *More Heat than Light: Economics as Social Physics: Physics as Nature's Economics*. Cambridge, MA: Cambridge University Press.
———. 2002. *Machine Dreams: Economics Becomes a Cyborg Science*. Cambridge, MA/New York: Cambridge University Press.
Mokyr, Joel. 2007. The Market for Ideas and the Origins of Economic Growth in Eighteenth Century Europe. *Tijdschrift voor Sociale en Economische geschiedenis* 4(1): 3.
Nisbet, Robert A. 1994. *History of the Idea of Progress*. New Brunswick: Transaction Publishers.
Pacioli, Luca. 1924. *Double-Entry Bookkeeping: An Original Translation of the Treatise on Double-Entry Bookkeeping*. Trans. P. Crivelli. London: Inst of Bookkeepers.
Rehmann, Jan. 2011. *Max Weber, Modernisation as Passive Revolution: A Gramscian Analysis, Historical Materialism*. Leiden: Brill.
Sandmo, Agnar. 2011. *Economics Evolving: A History of Economic Thought*. Princeton: Princeton University Press.
Schabas, Margaret. 2005. *The Natural Origins of Economics*. Chicago: University of Chicago Press.
Sedlacek, Tomas. 2011. *Economics of Good and Evil: The Quest for Economic Meaning from Gilgamesh to Wall Street*. New York/Oxford: Oxford University Press.
Shearer, R.A. 1961. The Concept of Economic-Growth. *Kyklos* 14(4): 497–532.
Singer, Kurt. 1958. Oikonomia: An Inquiry Into the Beginnings of Economic Thought and Language. *Kyklos* 11(1): 29–57.
Teggart, Frederick J. 1947. The Argument of Hesiod's Works and Days. *Journal of the History of Ideas* 8(1): 45–77.
Worster, Donald. 1994. *Nature's Economy: A History of Ecological Ideas, Studies in Environment and History*. 2nd ed. Cambridge, MA/New York: Cambridge University Press.

Chapter 6
The Meanings of Work in John Locke

Campbell Jones

The relation between work and property formulated by John Locke in the late seventeenth century has been of momentous historical significance. Joining others in calling into question the right to property seized by conquest or other extra-economic force – in short, property not exacted by human labour – Locke's ideas were crucial in the contestation of aristocratic privilege and played a key role in the structuring of modern claims to property. Against ideas of divine right, plunder and tradition, Locke's understanding of the relation between work and property proposed instead a rational equivalence of work and property. Claims to property could then only be justified by work.

The idea that property is justified by work holds out the promise of meritocracy based on effort. It certainly does not promise equality of property but instead promises an equality between work and property. Taking as a premise that some will choose to work harder and more industriously than others, this equivalence of work and property offers itself in the popular imagination and in economic and legal theory as the pinnacle of economic rationality and moreover equity and justice.

Locke's discussion of work and property in chapter five of his *Second Treatise of Government*, written in the early 1680s and published in 1690, remains a key source in justifications of private property rights. Much has been said about Locke's conception of property, and while what Locke says about the relation between work and property hinges on his conception of work, a rather significant set of problems arise if one pays close attention to the various and often inconsistent meanings of work in Locke. In this chapter I focus on the vacillation of the concept of work in Locke and draw out some of the consequences. This early modern referent point is important because, as has been widely argued, the twenty-first century is returning to forms of economic inequality characteristic of the eighteenth and nineteenth centuries (Piketty 2014). In this process, as inequalities of wealth and mechanisms by which

C. Jones (✉)
University of Auckland, Auckland, New Zealand
e-mail: campbell.jones@auckland.ac.nz

J. Bek-Thomsen et al. (eds.), *History of Economic Rationalities*, Ethical Economy 54, DOI 10.1007/978-3-319-52815-1_6

wealth expands capture public attention, these early modern justifications of wealth and property require close scrutiny as they creak and groan.

Criticisms of Locke's position on matters of political economy often treat this in isolation from the rest of his thought. This is perhaps unsurprising given that, as one of his great critics writes "it was the classical expression of the bourgeois society's ideas of right as against feudal society, and moreover his philosophy served as the basis for all the ideas of the whole of subsequent English political economy" (Marx 1861–1863, 367). It would be a risk however to underplay the importance in Locke's thought of religion, philosophy, medicine and natural science, and above all the way that his political economy is embedded in these. The breadth of his works makes this clear, as do the contents of his library at the time of his death, which shows a preponderance of works of theology and medicine and comprised only 10.7% works of politics and law and 3.5% works of economics (see Harrison and Laslett 1965, 18). Locke's writings on work and property need to be placed within the context of his other writings and his religious, philosophical and scientific as much as his political presuppositions.

Equally important is to locate Locke's writings firmly within the social context from which they emerge, without of course reducing them to that context. The social reading of Locke and of others has been masterfully deployed with important results by Neal Wood and Ellen Meiksins Wood. Following their work, a contextual reading attuned not only to the intellectual context of Locke's writings but also to its concrete historical situation is not to reduce Locke to being a mere reflex moment in that history. While he certainly was not a visionary proto-capitalist, placing Locke in the context of the development of capitalism enables positioning him within a series of very real social transformations and noting that "these social transformations generated conflicts over property in Locke's own time and place; and the issues at stake were very much the stuff of his ideas" (Wood 2012, 29).

Insofar as the social transformations of his and our times were and are contradictory, it is hardly surprising to find much that is contradictory in Locke. My first objective is to articulate some of the contradictions between several incompatible conceptions of work in Locke. In making such demonstrations it would be rash, as was claimed by Macpherson in his brilliant landmark reading of Locke, to argue that "however confused Locke may have been, he was not confused about the class structure of his own England" (Macpherson 1962, 216). It is also equally reductive, if not powerful in rhetorical flair, to argue that Locke "championed the new bourgeoisie in every way – he took the side of the manufacturers against the working classes and the paupers, the merchants against the old-fashioned usurers, the financial aristocracy against governments that were in debt; he even demonstrated in a separate work that the bourgeois way of thinking is the normal human way of thinking" (Marx 1859, 77). Locke's conception of work and his understanding of the relation between work and property are ultimately incoherent but, as I will seek to show, more important than that incoherence is the very specific effort made to paper over that incoherence with fundamentally religious and metaphysical notions about origin.

Of the many meanings of work in Locke, it is possible to identify at least four distinct concepts of work that contradict, contest and also interfere with and sometimes support one another. I will first identify the interplay between the ordinary or "vulgar concept of work" and the notion in Locke of "original labour." I will then discuss the place of the "labour of division" in relation to the understanding Locke has of "improved labour." Together these four concepts portend something of the vexed status of Locke's contradictory efforts to grapple with the meaning of work, and as such they cast a long shadow on the conceptions and realities of effort and its outcomes today.

6.1 Labour and Original Labour

Almost all discussions of work turn on what can be called the ordinary or "vulgar concept of work." On this conception, work is registered in the act of an individual at one moment of time, usually but not always acting directly on physical nature. Thus work can be captured almost photographically in a snapshot of the act of picking an apple or tilling a field. This vulgar concept of work plays a vital function in Locke, but I should emphasise that it does not play the role generally assigned to it, and further, that there are several other quite different conceptions of work in Locke, each bringing with them significantly different consequences.

While the vulgar concept of work was certainly not his invention, Locke routinely evokes it in his famous examples such as the collecting of acorns and gathering of apples. He generally immediately associates these acts with ownership. Thus, "He that is nourished by the acorns he picked up under an oak, or the apples he gathered from the trees in the wood, has certainly appropriated them to himself" (Locke 1690b, §28). The frequent appearance in Locke of this kind of example occludes the variety of other meanings of work in his writings, and in the absence in Locke of any explicit definition of work or labour, such examples can easily be taken as providing guidance or even a definition of what Locke means by work. In commentary on Locke, awareness of this problem or even an effort to explicitly clarify what Locke means by work or labour are notoriously lacking, even in the places where one would expect to find it (see, for example, Yolto 1993). Such definitional difficulties are glossed over largely because work as such is not taken as the focus but instead emphasis is put on the specific set of claims regarding property that are so promptly affixed to these examples of work. Given the interest and import of these claims, attention almost invariably turns to property and the relation between work and property. In doing so the meaning of work remains unspecified, and in the absence of specification it is almost always taken as read that Locke simply assumes the ordinary or vulgar concept of work.

Locke's claims about the relation of work and property, which on the surface amount to what is known as a "labour theory of property" proceed as follows. For Locke, "Though the earth, and all inferior creatures, be common to all men, every man has a *property* in his own *person*: this no body has any right to but himself. The *labour* of his body, and the *work* of his hands, we may say, are properly his" (Locke 1690b, §27). The activity of the person is the basis for the claim to exclusive property rights, on the basis that "he has mixed his *labour* with, and joined to it something that is his own, and thereby makes it his property" (1690b, §27). Again, in case the picture is not clear, Locke rephrases the point "this labor being the unquestionable property of the laborer, no man but he can have a right to what that is once joined to" (Locke 1690b, §27).

What is crucial here is the idea that labour is already an individual possession. Indeed, Macpherson argues that "his insistence that a man's labour was his own" is "the essential novelty of Locke's doctrine of property" (1962, 220). If this is important for this conception of property then it is even more so for his conception of work. For Locke: "man, by being master of himself, and *proprietor of his own person, and the actions or labour of it, had still in himself the great foundation of property*" (Locke 1690b, §44). There is here a perfect circle: work is the property of the individual, if there is equity then property is a result of work, ergo property is rightly the possession of that individual.

The specific examples Locke takes up here and elsewhere are attractive because of the way they appeal to the vulgar concept of work and further to the common sense of equity and justice in the idea that one who has worked has a higher claim on ownership than the one who has chosen idleness. Locke's argument indeed goes well beyond this simple notion of equivalence, but his examples appeal to common injunctions against idleness, that, as Max Weber reminds, were central to Lutheranism and Calvinism, often echoing the injunction of St Paul, whose writings occupied much of Locke's (1707) later years, that "The one who is unwilling to work shall not eat" (2 Thess. 3:10).

The plot thickens, however, when Locke admits that the "labour" that is performed at any actual moment of time need not necessarily be performed personally but can be done by an other. Indeed, one's "own" work might just as well be performed by an animal one owns or be the labour of a worker to whom I pay a wage. At this moment in time the activity of these things that are my property will themselves work, and moreover their labour will have issued not from them but from me, their owner. Thus:

> the grass my horse has bit, the turfs my servant has cut, and the ore I have digged in any place where I have a right to them in common with others, become my property without the assignation of consent of anybody. The labor that was mine, removing them out of that common state they were in, has fixed my property in them. (Locke 1690b, §28)

The labour of the horse or the servant justifies a property claim not for the horse or the servant but for their owner. It is worth noting that here again the vulgar concept of work is still at play, appearing in the snapshot moment of the horse, the cutter of turf or the miner. These are examples from the kind of work that Locke frequently observed others perform, even if he did not undertake this kind of work himself. Indeed, there is nothing random in the examples of the grazing of horses by which he so often travelled, the digging of turf that he witnessed in Holland and found more agreeable to his health than the coal burned in London, and the digging of ore which was undertaken by the peasants who rented from him the land in Somerset that he inherited from his father. What is most peculiar in Locke's image is not that the one who is supervising but not working has a right to the property produced, but that this property belongs to the overseer precisely *because* it is the product of *his* labour.

This makes sense in Locke because of the presence in his thought of a very specific idea of origin that runs deep through his thought. Recall that the stated purpose of the *Second Treatise* is to ascertain the true origin of civil government, as the purpose of the *Essay Concerning Human Understanding* is the inquiry into the origin of ideas. But the thematics of origin is a basic strategy in Locke's thought. This plays out across his writings on science and religion as much as his political economy. His theory of knowledge is grounded in the idea of original perception, which is the true basis of knowledge but is then covered up by the wordy obfuscations of metaphysics, scholasticism and bookishness, which are the "rubbish" that needs to be cleared away by sound observation of nature. Likewise his understanding of religion is that faith involves an immediate and original access to the truth that Jesus is the son of God, an original truth that is unnecessarily muddied by trivial debates about dogma and by the interference of state in religious practice and the impositions of above all Catholicism (Locke 1689). There are appearances, ideas and fine words, but the point again and again is that understanding ultimately traces back to an original unsullied experience.

As it is from original experience that understanding accrues, it is original labour to which property ultimately accrues. His is an argument from "natural law" and his economic ideas "have their Foundation in Nature, and are clear" (1695, 403). It should also further be remembered that Locke's problem in chapter five of the *Second Treatise* is the determination not of the right to property that comes from actual labour in the present but the original right to property. He is clear from the beginning to the end of chapter five that his goal is to determine "*how Labour could at first begin a Title of Property*" (Locke 1690b, §51). This theme of first beginnings is crucial. Locke's argument is that "*labour*, in the beginning, *gave a right of property*" (1690b, §45).

In Locke there are these first two competing meanings of work, although as we will see that there are at least two more. On the one hand work is the most palpably simple act of withdrawing physical matter from the state of nature in which it is held in common. This is a version of the vulgar concept of work. On the other hand, Locke lives in a specific society in which he is surrounded by others whose work is the material basis of his prosperity and others of his class but those workers do not, nor for him do they deserve to, share in that prosperity. What counts as work is therefore not the actual labour of the working class but rather an "original labour" that was undertaken in a mythical past by a hardworking few who have as a result a full right to the property they hold in the present. This myth of origin, which is taken as eminently practical and plays on the physical character of the examples given, presents itself as an antidote to metaphysical speculation and troublesome political claims. It is of course metaphysical through and through, rests on a specific economic claim that dismisses the work of others and furthermore assumes the incapacity of those workers to change their conditions.

6.2 The Labour of Division

While work is a visible presence in chapter five of the *Second Treatise*, playing out between the vulgar concept of work and the notion of original labour, in Locke's writings on money and interest work seems at first glance to disappear altogether. Turning to the sphere of circulation, it is no longer labour that is the sole source of value but rather "Trade" that is the "Foundation of Riches" (Locke 1692, 212). Locke assumes, with Aristotle and scholasticism, that money is not productive in its own right and therefore that usury preys on the more real work of others: "Money is a barren thing, and produces nothing, but by Compact transfers that Profit that was the Reward of one Man's Labour into another Man's Pocket" (Locke 1692, 250, see also 1668, 181).

Drawing a strict analogy between land and money and with this between rent and interest, he therefore finds that the principle which gives occasion to interest is nothing other than differences of wealth. Speaking of interest, he writes:

> That which occasions this, is the *unequal Distribution* of Money; which Inequality has the same effect too upon Land, that it has upon Money. For my having more Money in my Hand than I can, or am disposed to use in buying and selling, makes me able to lend: And another's want of so much Money as he could employ in Trade, makes him willing to borrow (Locke 1692, 250, see also 1668, 181–182)

Locke is more explicit than many today in explaining how deprivation can do a form of work in its own right as a means of inducement. As rent is a payment for admission to something from which one is legally excluded, so interest is the due cost of being excluded from wealth. Of this Locke concludes that "to Profit from the Loan of Money, is as equitable and lawful, as receiving Rent from Land, and more tolerable to the Borrower, notwithstanding the Opinion of some over-scrupulous Men" (1692, 251, see also 1668, 182–183).

There might seem to be a stark inconsistency between the labour theory of property from the *Second Treatise* and the explanation here of interest in terms of supply and demand. Indeed, ferreting out this inconsistency is a standard trope in many discussions of work and property in Locke. In his major study of capital and interest, for instance, Böhm-Bawerk proudly identifies this inconsistency in Locke: "On one occasion he [Locke] points out with great emphasis that labor is the source of all goods, and on another he calls interest a fruit of the labor of others" (1884, 242).

It should be stressed that this apparent inconsistency is already present in the *Second Treatise*, in which claiming for oneself the labour of others was, as we have seen, already clearly visible. Again, this problem can be covered over by introducing the element of time, and finding that property is ultimately justified by a more primal original labour. Set in play by an original division that is meritocratically established by work, unequal distribution then works as a *perpetuum mobile*, and for Locke any quarrelsome meddling with that purity of origin deserves to be dismissed as "overscrupulous." Work is therefore forever split in time for Locke between this mythical original labour and the palpably obvious labour of the working class from which Locke so visibly benefitted. Without this element of time and the ultimate recourse to original labour, it becomes hard to explain how Locke could hold such radically opposed positions on the value of human labour. On the one hand he holds that labour is the source of all legitimate claims to property and he will marvel at the products of work. On the other hand he will then treat the work of the overwhelming majority of human beings to be valued at precisely nothing. Here we can see rising what can properly be called the "labour of division."

It is clear that the creditor qua creditor does not work as such, and thus if a labour theory of property appears in the founding of property, the expansion of property through rent and interest takes place entirely outside the work of the rentier or usurer. Recall that for Locke there has been work in the past and it is that original labour which justifies rent and interest in the present. For Locke rent is the expropriation of the labour of others and this arises from the situation of want in which the borrower finds themself. This is justified again by the idea of an originary labour that in turn justifies the property that earns rent or the money that earns interest. In Locke we find not so much a labour theory of property as a *property theory of labour*. In short, what comes to be considered labour is that which has a claim on property. The theory is recursive, seeking to legitimate present conditions, and this contradiction continues through to the present day. Property is on this conception not so much a matter of possession as dispossession, a mechanism to derive advantage from unequal starting points. Labour then means strictly 'to divide' when it is said that "it is *labour* indeed that *puts the difference of value* on every thing" (1690b, §40).

Locke marvels at the fact that rents can be paid by tenant farmers who still produce profit. He argues that "all Encouragement should be given to the Artificers; and things so order'd, as much as might be, that those who make, should also Vend and Retail out their own Commodities" and he stresses "how much Manufacture deserves to be incourag'd" (Locke 1692, 241–242). In doing so, what is effecting "work" is now hardly a labourer at all, but rather the cunning of the way in which their work is arranged and a profit arises therefrom. What emerges here is that labour can be "improved," and thus a disjunction between simple labour and "improved labour."

Locke certainly does seem to rest on a vulgar conception of work when he writes that "Tis the number of people that make the riches of the country" (1693a, 487) or when he celebrates the increase of the number of the poor, arguing "If by pore are meant such as have noething to maintein them but their hands, Those who live by their labour are soe far from being a burthen that tis to them chiefly we owe our riches" (Locke 1693a, 491). It is because of the value that Locke puts on labour that he attacks what he calls "begging drones, who live unnecessarily upon other people's labour" (1697a, 448).

But at the same time, Locke fully recognises that vast improvements can be made to the productive capacities of labour. It has often been stressed that Locke put great value on work. Indeed he did write that "We ought to look on it as a mark of goodness in God that he has put us in this life under a necessity of labour" (1693b, 440). Not only is God the origin of the command of each and all to the work for which they have a calling, but God also operates as a principle of distinction, to reinforce the fact of the great difference between common human labour and the activity of

God. On the coversheet to the fourth edition of the *Essay Concerning Human Understanding* of 1700 Locke cites from Ecclesiastes: "thou knowest not the works of God, who maketh all things" (11:5). But if God is a being apart from human beings for Locke, what is more important regarding the question of the concept of work is that a quite different conception of work arises when one finds vast variability in the nature and results of various forms of human labour. Work for Locke is not an equal matter. For him, God gave the world to men, but not to all equally: "He gave it to the use of the industrious and rational (and *labour* was to be *his title* to it); not to the fancy or covetousness of the quarrelsome and contentious" (1690b, §34).

There seems indeed to be no outside of work for Locke, other than moral depravity, in "the relaxation of discipline, and corruption of manners" which are for him roughly equivalent with "vice and idleness" (Locke 1697a, 447). Recreation for him is something that needs be productive, as "unimproved land" that does not return a profit is pure waste. Taking his conception of recreation from Plato he advises against ill-spent leisure and advises "gentlemen" of the importance of not merely occupying themselves with study and books, but rather to learn an active diversion or recreation. Thus the value of taking up the learning of gardening, husbandry, delving, planting, inoculating, carpentry, joining, woodturning, perfuming, varnishing, engraving, working with precious stones and other "ingenious manual arts," not for their financial reward but for the physical benefits and health, alongside what is for Locke the quite natural benefit of being able to "govern and teach" one's staff (1693c, 153–157).

6.3 Improved Labour

The logic of improvement needs to be set within the context of the movement toward "improvement" of land in England in the sixteenth and seventeenth century, a dynamic that is central to Locke's thought (see Wood 1984, 2002, ch. 5). Locke is clear that "The Riches of the world doe not lye in haveing large tracts of good land which supplied abundantly the native conveniencys of Eating and drinking" but rather in trade, in manufacture and exchange, and that "In all manufactures the greatest part of the value lies in the labour" (Locke 1693a, 488).

Locke had a wide and varied interest in the variety of work and the ingenuity of the creative inventive uses of technology being progressively introduced into production in the time of his research, travel and writing. In his extensive travels through England, Germany, France and the Netherlands, Locke marvelled at the industry and ingenuity that he observed. In his travel, his reading, and his work for the Royal Society, the Board of Trade and Plantations and the Council of Trade, Locke saw the application of science to production and his practical attitude saw much of benefit in this. He kept extensive notes in particular on the creative and new methods of manufacture, being delighted for instance at his close friend Pointard's invention of a tapered glass bottle lid that might be used in the place of cork or wooden bottle stoppers. He wrote books on the techniques used in France for the cultivation and preservation of grapes, olives and fruit (Locke 1679) and a lengthy treatise on the history of navigation (Locke 1704).

Locke suffered under no illusions that work was inherently light or easy, nor that industry could not be "improved." In his 1697 proposal to the Council of Trade for the development of the manufacture and processing of linen in Ireland, for instance, he argued that instead of protecting England from wool imports, Ireland should improve the linen industry by specialisation and perfection. He proposed – with the exception of those with sufficient independent income from their estates – that all be induced toward spinning linen and advocated for the establishment of "spinning schools":

> to which all persons that have not forty shillings a year estate shall be obliged to send all their children, both male and female, that they have at home with them, from six to fourteen years of age, and may have liberty to send also those between four and six if they please, to be employed there in spinning ten hours in the day when the days are so long, or as it is light when they are shorter. (Locke 1697b, 366)

As with the application of science, this specialisation and "education" would lead to improvement of the productivity of labour. In this Locke departs markedly from the vulgar conception of work and the notion of original labour. This departure appears perhaps most tellingly toward the end of chapter five of the *Second Treatise* when he offers an account of the actual labour that goes into the production of a loaf of bread. In the course of arguing that "It is labor, then, which puts the greatest part of value upon land, without which it would scarcely be worth anything" (1690b, §43) he presents the vast array of labour involved in producing bread, which is worth quoting at length for the explicit recognition of the range of actors involved:

> it is not barely the ploughman's pains, the reaper's and thresher's toil, and the baker's sweat that is to be counted into the bread we eat; the labor of those who broke the oxen, who digged and wrought the iron and stones, who felled and framed the timber employed about the plough, mill, oven and any other utensils, which are a vast number requisite to this corn, from its being seed to be sown to its being made bread, must all be charged on the account of labor, and received as an effect of that; nature and the earth furnished only the most worthless materials as in themselves. It would be a strange 'catalogue of things that industry produced and made use of, about every loaf of bread' before it came to our use, if we could trace them: iron, wood, leather, bark, timber, stone, bricks, coals, lime, cloth, dyeing drugs, pitch, tar, masts, ropes, and all the materials made use of in the ship that brought any part of the commodities used by any of the workmen to any part of the work; all which it would be impossible, at least too long, to reckon up. (1690a, §43)

This account reappears nearly a century later in refined form at the end of the first chapter of book one of the *Wealth of Nations*, where Smith waxes lyrical about the fact the most basic clothing is produced by the "joint labour of a great multitude of workmen", noting the great variety of labour involved in producing simple commodities and of a workman "the different hands employed in preparing his bread and his beer", and that production involves the "assistance and cooperation of many thousands" (1776, 115–117). Echoing the impossible reckoning of labour in Locke, Smith writes that "the number of people of whose industry is a part, though but a small part, has been employed in procuring him this accommodation, exceeds all computation" (1776, 115).

Even in the *Second Treatise* which, as we have seen, is often wrongly assumed to rest on a vulgar concept of work when in fact the notion of original labour is pivotal, here arises the idea of fully socialised and improved labour. Locke marvelled at the computation and reckoning that would be required to acknowledge the work of others that had already become a reality in his time. He would then close his notebook and take his daily readings of the weather that he would publish with the Royal Society with the hope that one day such records might exist for the whole of England and beyond. He would pray and retire exhausted from his day of work.

6.4 Conclusion

The Locke that is usually taught today is one who insists on the importance of "clear and distinct" ideas and who offered an early modern defence of property grounded in labour. Here I have sought to draw attention to the fact that in Locke there is not one clear and distinct idea of work but rather at least four ideas of work that fold into one another, contradict one another and in doing so at times support one another. Such confusions may well keep Locke's texts alive and indeed sustain them, while they reflect deeper conflicts that play out beyond the covers of books.

Locke is early in the present dynamics by which economic holdings can by their own right lay claim to dispossession of others, a dynamic that is clearly central to the economic conflicts of the twenty-first century. Locke's property theory of labour is remarkably flexible, not only because it is circular but because the circle can be moved around in either direction. Taken one way it argues for a meritocracy of labour in which effort produces property. At the same time it advances a "meritocracy in reverse" in which the presumed equivalence of work and property means that the holder of property, however acquired, can justify that grasp because a presumed equivalence means that this property must have come about through hard or very clever work. When results can be easily quantified while the realities of work and its preconditions are unclear, it is easier to assume rather than to demonstrate such a relationship between work and property.

Locke's ideas clearly exceed their origin and have spread far and wide, and it is perhaps their dissemination that is more significant than their points of origin. Indeed, Locke's thought only makes sense if one concedes to it a set of presuppositions of origin, which play out in original unmediated access to the world and to God and a somehow originary labour that sets everything else in train. It is not just that Locke's position would not make much sense in a financialised economy premised on the logic of the derivative (Bryan and Rafferty 2006; LiPuma and Lee 2004; Martin 2015). The myth of origin that captivates Locke and his derivatives is not just an origin myth but rather an imposition that reads origin as more important than anything that comes later or from elsewhere. For Locke, in short, everything other is totally other.

Locke's thought and the forms of empiricism, liberalism and individualism that he inspired present themselves as an escape from metaphysics and mysticism. They find the grounds of their true religion and the origin of private property in a pure and original act. But this idea of pure origin, far from an escape from metaphysics is rather metaphysics itself. This is not just any metaphysics but a metaphysics of origin and moreover a religious metaphysics of origin in which the origin is always mysterious and unavailable to us fallen ones who are only of this world. If this metaphysics of origin speaks of what is, then what is appears, to it, as a mere supplement to something always more original.

Bibliography

Böhm-Bawerk, Eugen von. 1884/1959. *Capital and Interest, Volume 1: History and Critique of Interest Theories*. Trans. George D. Huncke and Hans F. Sennholz. South Holland: Libertarian Press.

Bryan, Dick, and Michael Rafferty. 2006. *Capitalism with Derivatives: A Political Economy of Financial Derivatives, Capital and Class*. Basingstoke: Palgrave MacMillan.

Harrison, John, and Peter Laslett. 1965. *The Library of John Locke*. Oxford: Oxford University Press.

LiPuma, Edward, and Benjamin Lee. 2004. *Financial Derivatives and the Globalization of Risk*. Durham: Duke University Press.

Locke, John. 1668/1991. Some of the Consequences that are Like to Follow Upon the Lessening of Interest to 4 per cent. In *Locke on Money*, ed. Patrick Hyde Kelly, Vol. 1. Oxford: Clarendon.

———. 1669/2003. The Fundamental Constitutions of Carolina. In *Political Writings*, ed. David Wooton. Indianapolis: Hackett.

———. 1679/1823. Observations Upon the Growth and Culture of Vines and Olives: The Production of Silk: The Preservation of Fruits. In *The Works of John Locke, in Ten Volumes*, Vol. 10. London: Thomas Tegg.

———. 1689/1983. *A Letter Concerning Toleration*, ed. James H. Tully. Indianapolis: Hackett.

———. 1690a/2004. *An Essay Concerning Human Understanding*, ed. Roger Woolhouse. London: Penguin.

———. 1690b/1980. *The Second Treatise of Government*, ed. C.B. Macpherson. Indianapolis: Hackett.

———. 1692/1991. Some Considerations of the Consequences of the Lowering of Interest, and Raising the Value of Money. In *Locke on Money*, ed. Patrick Hyde Kelly, Vol. 1. Oxford: Clarendon.

———. 1693a/1991. For a General Naturalization. In *Locke on Money*, ed. Patrick Hyde Kelly, Vol. 2. Oxford: Clarendon.

———. 1693b/2003. Labour. In *Political Writings*, ed. David Wooton. Indianapolis: Hackett.

———. 1693c/1996. Some Thoughts Concerning Education. In *Some Thoughts Concerning Education and Of the Conduct of the Understanding*, ed. Ruth W. Grant and Nathan Tarcov. Indianapolis: Hackett.

———. 1695/1991. Further Considerations Concerning Raising the Value of Money. In *Locke on Money*, ed. Patrick Hyde Kelly, Vol. 2. Oxford: Clarendon.

———. 1697a/2003. Draft of a Representation Containing a Scheme of Methods for the Employment of the Poor. In *Political Writings*, ed. David Wooton. Indianapolis: Hackett.

———. 1697b/1876. Encouragement of Irish Linen Manufacture. In *The Life of John Locke, in Two Volumes*, ed. H.R. Fox Bourne, Vol. 2. London: Henry King.

———. 1704/1823. The Whole History of Navigation from its Original to this Time. In *The Works of John Locke, in Ten Volumes*, Vol. 10. London: Thomas Tegg.

———. 1707/1987. *A Paraphrase and Notes on the Epistles of St Paul*, ed. Arthur W. Wainwright, Vol. 2. Oxford: Clarendon.

Macpherson, C.B. 1962/2011. *The Political Theory of Possessive Individualism: Hobbes to Locke*. Ontario: Oxford University Press.

Martin, Randy. 2015. *Knowledge Ltd: Toward a Social Logic of the Derivative*. Philadelphia: Temple University Press.

Marx, Karl. 1859/1970. *A Contribution to the Critique of Political Economy*. Moscow: Progress.

———. 1861–1863/1969. *Theories of Surplus Value, Part 1*. Trans. Emile Burns. London: Lawrence and Wishart.

Piketty, Thomas. 2014. *Capital in the Twenty-First Century*. Trans. Arthur Goldhammer. Cambridge, MA: Bellknap Press.

Smith, Adam. 1776/1986. *The Wealth of Nations, Books I-III*, ed. Andrew Skinner. London: Penguin.

Weber, Max. 1904–1905/1992. *The Protestant Ethic and the Spirit of Capitalism*. Trans. Talcott Parsons. London: Routledge.

Wood, Neal. 1983. *The Politics of Locke's Philosophy: A Social Study of An Essay Concerning Human Understanding*. Berkeley: University of California Press.

———. 1984. *John Locke and Agrarian Capitalism*. Berkeley: University of California Press.

Wood, Ellen Meiksins. 2002. *The Origin of Capitalism: A Longer View*. London: Verso.

———. 2012. *Liberty and Property: A Social History of Western Political Thought from Renaissance to Enlightenment*. London: Verso.

Yolto, John W. 1993. *A Locke Dictionary*. Oxford: Blackwell.

Chapter 7 Financial Reasoning in The Midst of Revolution and Wars: Merchants and Bankers Between Paris, London, and Amsterdam, 1789–1810

Niccolò Valmori

7.1 Economic Reasoning and Political Constraints: Thomas Coutts and Francis Baring During French Revolutionary Wars (1792–1801)

In this section I mainly deal with two members of the financial community of London during the troublesome period of the Revolutionary wars: Thomas Coutts and Francis Baring. More specifically, I consider how their personal understanding of the political situation in Europe affected the business decisions taken by them and to what extent, the instability of the continent modified their portfolios, causing them to move into new fields of investment.

The two London bankers exemplified perfectly the two poles of the London market. On the one hand, Coutts was a private banker, whose main business was lending money to the most eminent members of the aristocracy, included the Royal family; on the other hand, Francis Baring was one of the first merchant bankers to establish himself and his family in the highest ranks of the London financial community.

At the end of the eighteenth century, the London financial market was already shaped by the distinction between bankers whose main interest was in lending money to members of the aristocracy and profiting on the interest produced by this activity, and those who did not neglect speculation on goods and government funds. This distinction emerged also in the different London locations of the banks: those bankers more active in investing money coming from landowners resided in the West End, Fleet Street and the Strand, whereas bankers and brokers with interest in trade speculation and maritime assurance had their headquarters in the City clustered around Lombard Street (Joslin 1954).

N. Valmori (✉)
European University Institute, Florence, Italy
e-mail: niccolo.valmori@eui.eu

J. Bek-Thomsen et al. (eds.), *History of Economic Rationalities*, Ethical Economy 54, DOI 10.1007/978-3-319-52815-1_7

The interest in stock investment and financial speculation was rapidly spreading beyond the small world of brokers and bankers as signalled by the large diffusion of manuals and publications dedicated to the financial operations. In this massive stream of printed works two books stood out for their success and originality: *Every man his own broker* by Thomas Mortimer and *The Stocks examined and compared: or a Guide to purchasers in the Public Funds* by William Fairman. Mortimer's book was published fourteen times, becoming a well-established best seller for anyone interested in the Stock Exchange. Its expressed aim was to offer a handbook on stock trading in order to reduce the power of stockbrokers (Mortimer 1785). The appeal of the British funds went well far beyond the country's borders, whetting the appetite of many foreign investors, in particular Dutch investors.

Until the outbreak of the Fourth Anglo-Dutch war (1780–1784), the relationship between the two market places of Amsterdam and London was so close that when in 1763 a series of bankruptcies occurred among Amsterdam firms, English houses of trade helped their correspondents with large remittances (Riley 1973).

Amsterdam merchant houses, such as Hogguer, Van Staphorst, De Smith, and Hope, were specialized in dealing with launching loans in the name of foreign monarchies, ranging from England to Russia. Since Due to endless state of war between the main eighteenth-century powers of the European political system, monarchies needed large sums of money to pay their troops as well as bills of exchange acceptable in foreign countries. To this particular need many Amsterdam houses of commerce offered their services in exchange for a commission which ranged between 4 and 9% of the entire sum lent to the government. Once the Amsterdam banker and the foreign monarch had reached agreement, the banker gave the order to trusted brokers to offer part of the loan to interested investors in the Amsterdam market (Neal and Carlos 2011).

Dutch investors, though traditionally linked to the British securities market, started to reduce their presence in the London Stock market not only for political reasons, such as the war between the Netherlands and England, but also because other securities offered more advantageous terms, as was the case, for example, for the French annuities.

The Parisian Stock Exchange offered a wide variety of financial products that attracted an increasing number of foreign investors: Dutch and Swiss bankers were enticed by annuities circulating on the French market, which yielded incredibly high interest rates to the investors. The most interesting product was the *rente viagère* (life annuity), which could yield up to 8–10% interest per year, and could be assigned to young people thus assuring longer duration of profits for the capitalist who bought them (Velde 1995). This market offered countless opportunities as life annuities were launched to finance the ever-growing debt of the French Crown, which deepened after the active participation of France in the American War of Independence.

Thomas Coutts was member of a Scottish family active in trade and rapidly attracted by the opportunities available on the London market. In 1761, Thomas joined his brother James in a partnership, which lasted for 15 years; then in 1775 the bank became known as Thomas Coutts & Co. In the following years Coutts opened the partnership to two brokers Edmund and John Antrobus and then to his nephew John (Healey 1992). What made the fortune of Coutts and his firm was the personal friendship that linked the Scottish banker with his countryman Lord Bute.

Bute was a mentor of George III, and for a short period (1762–1763) was his Prime Minister. Due to this connection, Coutts became the banker in charge of the Privy Purse of which the main duty was the administration of the personal income of the sovereign and his family. Having reached this outstanding position, Coutts rapidly enlarged his clientele, which included relevant members of the English political scene such as William Pitt the Elder and Wiliam Pitt the Younger, the Duke of Wellington, and the Foreign Secretary, Lord Grenville.

At the outbreak of the French Revolution, Coutts did not seem alarmed by news coming from France, considering that this would not impair the good trend of the British funds. As a matter of fact the London banker believed that the English economy could at last grow in peace and restore the prosperity interrupted by the American War. Coutts did not foresee the gathering of the revolutionary storm, which would strike England as well as the Continent, and he was still confident in the recovery of the English economy during the spring of 1792, notwithstanding the outbreak of the war between France and the Austrian Empire.[1] At first, the banker did not take into account the rapid political evolution on the continent as something that could have a devastating impact on the British market.

When England also became directly involved in the continental wars against revolutionary French troops, the effect on the internal British credit market was particularly negative since the intervention of England in Europe significantly increased the public debt and made access to credit more difficult for small country merchants who usually borrowed money from the London market. The only way out for Coutts from this general credit crunch was to limit as much as possible any credit to unknown borrowers or to clients related to country banks that were experiencing bank runs.

The attitude of the banker towards the war was twofold: on the one hand he could not help supporting all the measures enacted by Pitt's government to provide for the British military efforts in Europe; on the other hand, he hoped that England might learn from this war not to intrude ever again in European conflicts, which were extremely burdensome for the public finances and therefore counterproductive for the entire economy. Coutts did not disapprove in principle of public expenditure for military reasons but he wanted to limit this to the improvement of the navy to act as a wall between England and Europe.

It is clear that Coutts analysed the political situation produced by the revolutionary wars from an economic perspective. His doubtful support of the military effort

[1] Coutts' optimism concerning the British economy was undoubtly due to the speech of William Pitt at the House of Commons on 17th February. In this speech the Prime Minister announced the existence of a surplus that could be vested in the reduction of the public debt. It was in that occasion that William Pitt pronounced one of the most unfortunate prophesy: "Unquestionably there never was a time in the history of this country, when, from the situation of Europe, we might more reasonably expect fifteen years of peace, than we may at the present moment" (Cobbett 1820).

put in place by England was in consequence of his economic reasoning on benchmarks such as the rise of the public debt and the soundness of the credit market. Coutts' reasoning appeared to be well founded: the Government postponed the payment of its officers and at the same time a dire credit crisis stroke the entire country when on 17th February 1797 Bank of England suspended her specie payments. However, the Scottish banker could not always follow his "economic reasons" because he had also to face political constraints resulting from being the personal banker of Lord Grenville.

Lord Grenville had been appointed Secretary at the Foreign Office in 1791 and from his personal bank account he supported all English agents abroad and funded all opponents of the French revolution all over Europe. In other words, Coutts was informally in charge of payments to English agents engaged by the Foreign Office in counterrevolutionary activities in Europe. This prestigious and secret office burdened Coutts with many unpleasant practices such as bills of exchange refused, overdrawing by his clients and endless practices of credit recovery. Coutts was not the only banker who supported with his funds covert operations aimed to weaken French interest in Europe (Durey 2009). Together with this charge, Coutts credited money to Foreign Office members who resided abroad. This last activity was not safer than the former: it took him 5 years to recover more than £2500 that he had lent to the former ambassador at Warsaw who had kept drawing on Coutts without having funds.

Thomas Coutts & Co. lived a paradoxical development: on the one hand, it restrained all its credit activities even with long-term clients, on the other hand it gained an important position within the government finances, particularly by being the personal banker of the Foreign Secretary. The decision to restraining credit activities while waiting for better times was not the only way open to bankers as is shown by the case of Baring brothers & C. which will be described in the following paragraphs.

The Baring family had been active in the textile trade since the second half of the eighteenth century (Ziegler 1988). Their first establishment was in the city of Exeter from where Francis moved to London to open a new branch in the capital. Rapidly Francis Baring eclipsed his two brothers, John and Charles, and established the firm under the name of Francis Baring & Co. as one of the main houses of commerce in Europe. At the outbreak of the first French war Francis Baring sat on the Board of Directors of the East India Company, and in the House of Commons, and had been created a baronet.

The high social status reached by its founder was not enough to avoid Francis Baring & Co. being affected by the continental wars as one of its most relevant partners was the Dutch firm Hope & Co. and the troublesome state of affairs in Europe endangered all speculative trade in goods which was the main field of activity for the British bank. Nonetheless, it was during this precise period that Francis Baring & Co. decided to risk new investments whereas the majority of the other bankers limited their activities, as has been showed in the case of Coutts.

Francis Baring sent his young son Alexander to the United States to evaluate the possible profitability of a large land purchase in Maine. Alexander Baring had had his apprenticeship at the Hope office in Amsterdam, which he had to leave when the French armies invaded the country, and his new mission to America consisted of checking closely the value of the investment proposed to Baring and Hope to acquire large portions of land in Maine. The correspondence between father and son offered a unique perspective not only on the economical reasons behind the choices of the bank but also of the political understanding of the American society seen through the eyes of the young Baring.

When Baring arrived at the end of 1795, land prices were already skyrocketing as a result of high European demand. He also noted that interest rates on some commercial bills reached 12% per year, showing how insecure was the American market, which not surprisingly was marked by a series of bankruptcies. In this case, the young Baring proposed to invest capital in American market in the name of the political soundness of the system. In other words, it can be said that a large capital investment was more the outcome of political consideration rather than the consequence of good economic signs.

Baring was particularly confident about the political system of the United States, emphasizing the merits of its constitution, which would enable the country to experience a peaceful transition from the Washington presidency to his successor. The solidity of the federal government largely overcame the divisions between parties and thus assured Baring that investments in land property in the United States would be under the protection of the federal government, whatever the party ruling the country. Alexander reassured his father that the political differences between the Federalist party, led by John Adams and Alexander Hamilton, and the Republican party, led by Thomas Jefferson and James Madison, did not concern in any circumstances the protection of property owned by foreigners.

Furthermore, news coming from London reported the dire situation of the credit market, which was dangerously close to a total credit crunch. This credit crisis was read by Alexander Baring as an opportunity to spread his risk and to diversify his portfolio with larger investments in the United States. Therefore, after the large investments in land estate, Alexander Baring started to focus his attention on another field of investment: the American security market.

Alexander Baring suggested that his father and Hope invest largely in different American stocks without neglecting the Bank stock which even though more volatile than the others could offer generous dividends, up to 12% per year. Following Alexander's tips the American market swiftly became as one of the most relevant sectors of investment for Baring & Co. (Austin 2007). The risky move to invest capital in the American market in the midst of the troubled period of the Revolutionary wars would pay dividends in the long term.

7.2 Hottinguer and His Dutch Clients: The Forced Diversification of Investment (1801–1807)

In this section I consider the case of Jean-Conrad Hottinguer, a Swiss banker resident in Paris, as a privileged point of observation on the world of Dutch investors in the period of the Napoleonic Empire. The career of Jean-Conrad Hottinguer epitomizes the successful banker able to read market evolutions as well as political turnabouts in not only on economic terms. Jean-Conrad Hottinguer was born in 1764 in Zurich where he started his apprenticeship as a bookkeeper for his uncle. Later he moved to Paris where he started to work in the financial house of Lecouteulx & C. After this experience in a well-known French house of commerce, Hottinguer moved to work with another Swiss banker, Denis Rougemont. Rapidly, Hottinguer became Rougemont's partner but as such he came close to failure when Rougemont went into bankruptcy for a badly conceived speculation on colonial goods in 1792 (Gérard 1972).

After a short period in Zurich, where he had escaped from Paris - where the Terror imposed by Jacobin authorities openly persecuted foreign bankers – he decided to seek a safe refuge in the United States where he remained until the beginning of the Directory.

From a study of notarial documentation concerning Hottinguer's activity during Napoleonic Empire, it emerges that Dutch clients kept playing an important role in the business run by the Swiss banker. The persistent relevance of Dutch capital on the Parisian stock exchange is the clear sign of a twofold development: on the one hand Dutch capital remained significant even after the partial decline of Amsterdam as a financial centre, on the other hand, the weighty investments made by Dutch firms in the French debt signalled the attempt of Paris to become a truly European stock exchange during the first years of the nineteenth century.

An analysis of the notarial documentation shows that Hottinguer's Dutch clients were mainly interested in the French public debt. In 1793 the *Grand Livre de la dette public* was created to offer a solid guarantee to the creditors of the State that all obligations made by previous government would be lawfully executed. However in 1797, the situation of public finance remained critical and forced the Directory into partial default in order to be able to pay at least one third of the entire debt. Moreover, it was stated that all French bonds could yield a 5% interest and not more as it was the case before this reform, euphemistically called "consolidation of one third," but more generally known as the "bankruptcy of the two thirds."

Hottinguer's Dutch clientele was composed of some small merchants, but also of important bankers such as Voombergh, Halmael and Borski, and Van Staphorst, Willink & Co. These two banks specialized in dealing with foreign loans, especially the placement of American bonds for the European buyers. The Swiss banker became the agent of Voomberg, Halmael and Borski from the winter 1805. Voombergh, Haelmael and Borski, who constitued a bank syndicate, entrusted to Hottinguer one task: to sell their French bonds that were registered in the Great Book of the Public Debt.

During the period taken into consideration, there were times when Hottinguer received a higher number of sell orders than at other times when his Dutch peers seemed less interested in selling their French bonds. An example of this swift changes in the sell orders is given by the spring 1807: Hottinguer had received sell orders for a value of 178,000 francs during the entire month of April and the first half of May whereas just in the week from 20th to 27th May Hottinguer was asked to sell French bonds for a value of 676,000 francs.

What led Voomberg and his associate to sell in 1 week an amount of bonds valued three times and a half their sell orders of the previous month and a half? The most-likely reason to explain these financial operations can be found in the news of the opening of a loan in favour of Spain on the Dutch market. This loan was imposed by the Emperor Napoleon who was waiting for the payment of the sum due by Spain to France: since the Spanish Crown could not find the capital, it turned to the Dutch market. After the direct pressure of the French Foreign minister, on 21st May 1806, the king Louis Bonaparte gave the order to open a loan in favour of Spain. Therefore, the decision to sell so many French bonds seems correlated with the necessity to have enough capital for the new loan.

This case shows how political decisions interfered with previous economic choices, but did not necessary ruin economic perspectives of bankers open to new risks and opportunities. Moreover this episode nuanced the image of a swift decline of the Amsterdam financial market during the period of the Napoleonic Empire. There were no doubts that the new Kingdom of Holland had lost many capitals fled abroad already during the period of the Batavian Republic. Nonetheless, Amsterdam maintained its role of financial hub for all satellite kingdoms that needed to borrow money in order to pay the high indemnities imposed by Napoleon.

7.3 Conclusions

Rather then following the traditional path of analysis, modelled on the paradigm of the rise and fall of financial centres (Spufford 2006), I have shown how some distinguished bankers directed their business in consequence of the political events taking place in England or in the continental Europe. At the core of this paper is the understanding of the reasoning behind certain investment choices during the period of revolutionary wars. It emerges how political choice interacted with economic reasoning on risks and opportunities, new investments, trust and doubt. In all the cases discussed, bankers faced the same challenge: they need to enlarge their perspectives to include political development abroad as well as at home.

The English case offers a perfect example of how from similar analysis of the political scenario, diverging investment decisions may be made. Thomas Coutts and Francis Baring agreed on the analysis of the deep impact of British involvement in European conflicts on the credit market, the availability of capital, and the general welfare of London stock market. However, they decided to follow two divergent paths to escape from the economic crisis at the end of eighteenth century: whereas

Coutts decided to restrict his credit activities not only to possible clients but also to his long-term clients, Francis Baring sent his son to follow closely the American market, including that of land speculation as well as of attractive stocks.

The different decisions cannot be explained just as the result of the different temperaments of the two bankers or as a choice between a more secure and a riskier way to approach the market. I assume that the different visions of investment are more related to the fact that Baring and Coutts belonged to two different branches of bankers which differed not just in their labels, merchant banker and private banker, but also from the way of envisioning ways out from the economic crisis. The clear distinction between the two bankers resulted in the presence or absence of a key concept: the diversification of the portfolio. Thus, Alexander Baring invited his father to extend investments in the United States to create a security in the case of a collapse of the British market; whereas Thomas Coutts justified his restrictive credit policy as the only way to preserve the stability of his bank.

Hottinguer could survive through the troubled period of the French revolution due to his understanding of the upcoming persecutions against moneyed men under the Jacobins rule. Once he returned to Paris he had a large network of clients going beyond the Parisian market. The Swiss banker profited from his links with various Dutch houses of commerce and he did not miss the opportunity to represent their interest in the French securities as well as into the loans that satellite kingdoms like Spain and Portugal issued on the Amsterdam market.

Bibliography

Archival sources: National Archives at Kew Gardens (PRO 30/8/29/2); Baring Archives (Maine Papers); National Archives in Paris (AN, ET XV).

Austin, Peter E. 2007. *Baring Brothers and the Birth of Modern Finance*. London: Pickering & Chatto.

Carter, Alice. 1953. Dutch Foreign Investment, 1738–1800. *Economica* 20: 322–340.

Cobbett, William. 1806–1820. *Parliamentary History of England: From the Norman Conquest, in 1066, to the Year 1803*. London: R. Bagshaw.

Coleridge, Ernest Hartley. 1920. *The Life of Thomas Coutts, Banker*. London/New York: John Lane, John Lane Company.

Cope, S.R. 1978. The Stock Exchange Revisited: A New Look at the Market in Securities in London in the Eighteenth Century. *Economica* 45: 3–7.

Durey, Michael. 2009. *William Wickham, Master Spy: The Secret War Against the French Revolution*. London: Pickering & Chatto.

Gérard, Max. 1972. *Messieurs Hottinguer, banquiers à Paris*. Paris: Draeger frères.

Healey, Edna. 1992. *Coutts & Co 1692–1992: The Portrait of a Private Bank*. London: Hodder & Stoughton.

Hidy, Ralph W. 1970. *The House of Baring in American Trade and Finance; English Merchant Bankers at Work, 1763–1861*. New York: Russell & Russell.

Joslin, D.M. 1954. London Private Bankers, 1720–1785. *The Economic History Review* 7: 167–186.

Mortimer, M. 1785. *Everyman His Own Broker*. London: Robinson.

Neal, Larry. 1990. *The Rise of Financial Capitalism: International Capital Markets in the Age of Reason*. Cambridge, MA/New York: Cambridge University Press.
Neal, Larry, and Ann M. Carlos. 2011. Amsterdam and London as Financial Centers in the Eighteenth Century. *Financial History Review* 18: 21–46.
Riley, James C. 1973. Dutch Investment in France 1781–1787. *The Journal of Economic History* 33: 732–760.
Robinson, Ralph M. 1929. *Coutts', the History of a Banking House*. London: J. Murray.
Spufford, Peter. 2006. From Antwerp and Amsterdam to London: The Decline of Financial Centres in Europe. *De Economist* 154: 143–175.
Velde, François. 1995. Macroeconomic Features of the French Revolution. *Journal of Political Economy* 103: 474–518.
Velde, François, and David W. Weir. 1992. The Financial Market and Government Debt Policy in France, 1746–1793. *Journal of Economic History* 52: 1–39.
White, Eugene N. 1995. The French Revolution and the Politics of Government Finance, 1770–1815. *Journal of Economic History* 55: 227–255.
Ziegler, Philip. 1988. *The Sixth Great Power Barings 1762–1929*. London: Collins.

Chapter 8
Prose Genre and the Emergence of Modern Economic Reasoning in Eighteenth-Century Britain

Jill Marie Bradbury

8.1 Introduction

> There is nothing which requires more to be illustrated by Philosophy than does trade.
> (Samuel Johnson, *Boswell's Life of Johnson*)

Historians of economic thought typically identify the eighteenth century as the moment when scientific approaches to the subject first emerged. This is usually taken to mean two things. First, that certain writers developed a modern notion of the economy as a system of interrelated components and forces governed by natural laws. Second, that they incorporated elements of empiricist methodology, including structure of argument and kinds of evidence. The economy emerged as an object of knowledge and political economy as a discourse not merely distinct from, but superior to political, religious, and cultural modes of reasoning. These developments are tied to the gradual displacement of scholastic/deductive/a priori methodologies by empiricist/inductive/a posteriori ones during the seventeenth and eighteenth centuries. William Letwin, Deborah Redman, and Margaret Schabas, among others, have adeptly demonstrated the influence of modern scientific rationalities on the evolution of political economy. I would like supplement their work by drawing attention to how these debates about the nature of scientific knowledge were also about the nature of language and discourse in general, and textual genre in particular. In brief, I argue that economic rationality itself came into being through the emergence of a specific form of prose narrative. To see this, we must consider: (a) how empiricist scientific discourse engaged with issues of linguistic and textual representation; (b) how these concerns influenced early writings on economic topics; (c) how a certain

J.M. Bradbury (✉)
Department of English, Gallaudet University, Washington, DC, USA
e-mail: jill.bradbury@gallaudet.edu

J. Bek-Thomsen et al. (eds.), *History of Economic Rationalities*, Ethical Economy 54, DOI 10.1007/978-3-319-52815-1_8

genre of these writings, identified by a particular structure of argument and use of rhetoric, came to be identified as "scientific" and, therefore, authoritative, in the eighteenth century.

8.2 Transitioning to Early Modern Conceptions of Science and Language

Ephraim Chambers' *Cyclopaedia; or An universal dictionary of arts and sciences* defined science as a system "orderly and artfully laid down in words" (1738, ix). This statement encapsulates the centrality of language and textual representation to scientific philosophy in the seventeenth and eighteenth centuries. As R. F. Jones commented many years ago, "It is hard to overemphasize the fact that science in its youth considered the linguistic problem as important as the problem of the true scientific method" (1951, 157). Scholastic thinkers conceptualized the natural world as a system of signs and scientific inquiry as a process of interpreting this language. The new empiricist paradigms rejected this hermeneutic model and, with it, the assumption of an essential homology between words and nature. This raised the problem of language mediating between the mind and "things themselves." If words lack a stable referent, whether in phenomenal reality or in the mind, nothing regulates their signification or ensures that they express sensorial perceptions adequately and exactly. The new empiricists were thus often concerned with the relationship between linguistic/textual representation and knowledge of the natural world.

Francis Bacon's "new science" proposed a model of knowledge that would introduce a "real and solid inquiry according to the laws of nature, not language" (1863, 8:476). Empirical phenomena and experimental observations were to be collected in the narratives of natural history, which would then be abstracted into "tables of presentation," then into axioms, and so on up to the realm of metaphysics. These materials would form the primary history, a comprehensive survey of the state of human knowledge. The natural histories had to be written concisely and without stylistic flourishes, for these "aim at the heights of speech, rather than the subtleties of things," thereby contributing to the mind's distortion of nature (8:476). Rhetoric does, however, have a key epistemological function. Along with logic, rhetoric is "the gravest of sciences, being the arts of arts," and Bacon attributed both epistemological and ethical functions to it (8:402). The use of rhetoric enables the imagination to protect the understanding from the "juggleries of words" and the "violence of the passions" (9:131). "Rhetoric is the only tool, Bacon posited, which can prevent the passions from forming a confederacy with the imagination, to the everlasting disadvantage of reason and the advancement of learning" (Stephens 1972, 258). Bacon's reflections on the relationship between knowledge, language and discourse also touched on the classification of the natural histories and other forms of textual communication. In the *Preparative Towards a Natural and Experimental History* and The *Advancement of Learning*, Bacon followed classical and medieval theories in using faculty psychology as the basis for his schemas. Thus, "History has reference to the Memory, poesy to the Imagination, and philosophy to the Reason" (1863, 8:407). These general modes of discourse were broken down into particular genres, such as theology and moral philosophy, or civil and natural history, on the basis of both subject matter and manner of representation.

The foundation of Bacon's *Novum Organum* was experentia literata. Without textual form, the "excellent liquor of knowledge" would be lost (8:397); without the genre of natural history, "no progress worthy of the human race could have been made or can be made in the philosophies and the sciences" (8:354). Carefully defined words, appropriate rhetorical style, and properly structured narratives were essential to the discovery of scientific truths through empirical observation and induction. Later exponents of empiricism, however, took a more negative view of the relationship between linguistic representation and scientific knowledge. In the late seventeenth century, Robert Boyle, Samuel Hartlib, William Petty, and Isaac Newton all composed proposals for language reform that sought to create the hylomorphism between words and nature that scholastic intellectual paradigms had assumed (Knowlson 1975, 8). Most scientists and philosophers associated with the English empirical tradition came to reject Bacon's views on the productive capacity of textual discourse and the epistemological importance of rhetoric. In *An Essay Concerning Human Understanding* (1689), John Locke asserted that, "if we would speak of things as they are, we must allow that all the art of rhetoric, besides order and clearness; all the artificial and figurative applications of words eloquence hath invented, are for nothing else but to insinuate wrong ideas, move the passions, and thereby mislead the judgment" (1959, 2:146). Thomas Sprat's 1667 *The History of the Royal Society* aimed to separate "the knowledge of Nature from the colours of Rhetorick, the devices of Fancy, or the delightful deceit of Fables" (1958, 62), and to protect it from "luxury and redundancy of speech" (111). For Sprat, rhetoric incited the passions and distracted the understanding from its observation of pure sensory impressions. Scientific discourse should thus not partake of figurative language: "Whereas the intention of ours, being not the Artifice of words, but a bare knowledge of things; my fault may be esteemed the less, that I have written of philosophy without any ornament of eloquence" (40).

8.3 Transitioning to New Concepts of Prose Discourse

At the same time proponents of empiricism were wrestling with the complexities of linguistic representation, the cognitive role of rhetorical style, and the transmission of knowledge in prose form, the field of textual production itself was profoundly changing. The seventeenth century saw an explosion of print, as technology improved, the price of paper dropped, government censorship relaxed, and literacy rates increased. New forms emerged, such as newspapers, periodical magazines, travel narratives, and novels. Writers experimented with the new possibilities of prose, mixing techniques and forms from different genres of writing or inventing new ones altogether. Existing classificatory schemes, which identified philosophy, poetry, and history as the main categories of oral discourse and a small number of distinct compositional genres for each, became outmoded. Publisher booklists from the late seventeenth century illustrate the difficulties of defining genres of prose in the new print culture. John Starkey's 1672 catalog divided publications into Divinity, Physick, Law, History, Poetry, and Plays, while William Thackeray's 1689 trade list used the classifications small godly books, small merry books, double books, and histories (McKeon 1987, 26). The idiosyncratic nature of such genres attests to the cognitive dissonance wrought by the sudden expansion of prose texts. It would not have been easy for contemporary readers to categorize the new print forms they encountered as scientific, historical, philosophical, or imaginative discourse, for such distinctions were themselves in transition.

8.4 The Proper Genre for Economic Writings – Representational Choices and Analytic Modes

Given this context of seismic changes in scientific epistemology and textual production, people who wrote about economic topics in the late seventeenth and early to mid-eighteenth centuries frequently engaged with issues of language, rhetoric and genre. One way these writers explored the representational nature of their work was through experimentation with textual forms and narrative voice. The dialogue was frequently employed, as in *England's Great Happiness, or a Dialogue between Content and Complaint* (1677). The anonymous author of this treatise also opened with a poem, "The Author to His Book." The 1683 pamphlet *Bank Credit, or the Usefulness and Security of the Bank of Credit Examined* is also framed as a dialogue between a country gentleman and a London merchant. Other popular forms of exposition included letters to friends and responses to sermons. Both the dialogue and letter allowed for the adoption of personas and other techniques of imaginative composition. Daniel Defoe and Jonathan Swift wrote popular expositions of economic issues that integrated imaginative narrative and philosophical argument. Defoe's *Robinson Crusoe* has much in common with the economic themes and ideas he proposed in *A Plan of the English Commerce* (1728). Swift's *Drapier's Letters* (1724) used fictional techniques to elucidate monetary theory, but he also published works outlining general economic principles, such as *Maxims Controlled in Ireland* (c. 1728). A final example of experimentation with textual form, one that has not been consigned to the dust bin of the history of economic thought, is George Berkeley's *The Querist* (1735).

Some early tracts and treatises on economic issues reflected on their own representational strategies by considering problems of rhetoric. However inconsistently carried out, William Petty's intention to discuss economic topics in terms of "number, weight, and measure" aligned with the critique of language in the new theories of science. In 1680, William Petyt prefaced his treatise *Britannia Languens, Or A*

Discourse of Trade with a rejection of rhetorical argument: "Trade being a matter of business, and the business of the ordinary people, at least, equally with the rest; I have not endeavored to dress it up with Curiosity of Phrases, by conforming myself to the Laconick or Ciceronian way, by studying for Metaphors, spruce words, or the renowned Antithesis; nor do I find these flowers will very aptly mingle with the Notions of Trade" (McCulloch 1954, 277–278). The preface to Dudley North's *Discourses Upon Trade* (1691), written by his brother, Roger, also began with an extensive discussion of the appropriate style for writing about money and trade. The author's decision to publish this work anonymously is attributed to his unwillingness to polish his discourse "into such accurate Method, and clean Style, as the World commonly expects from Authors." In place of "Neatness and Dress," he has relied "wholly upon the Truth and Justice of his Matter" (i). The propensity of rhetoric to create ambiguity in striving for "Elegance of Expression" is also mentioned (ii). And in *Considerations on the East India Trade* (1701), Henry Martyn borrowed directly from Petty in describing his attempt "to express himself in Terms of Number, Weight, and Measure," rather than "comparative and superlative Words to amuse the Reader" (McCulloch 1954, 543).

Finally, some late seventeenth and early eighteenth-century writers on economic topics broached the problem of genre by laying claim to the authority of scientific argument. Petty described his analysis of Irish socio-economics as proceeding "without recourse to the Authority of Story, but rather diligently observing the Law and Course of Nature" (Hull 1899, 1:204). North explained his *Discourses Upon Trade* (1691) as a consideration of "trade in general, upon true principles" and using a "method of reasoning … introduced with the new philosophy" (v–vi). John Cary began *A Discourse on Trade* (1717) by observing that "Trade has its principles, as other sciences have" (1). Isaac Gervaise characterized the aim of *The System or Theory of the Trade of the Whole World* (1720) as seeking out first causes, "such Principles, as seem to me capable of answering any Event in Trade" (iv). Richard Cantillon's *Essay on the Nature of Commerce in General* (c. 1730, p. 1755) criticized Petty as "fanciful and remote from natural laws, because he has attached himself not to causes and principles, but only to effects" (Brewer 2001, 21). In his 1740 treatise, *Representation Concerning the Knowledge of Commerce as a National Concern*, Joseph Massie explicitly connected the question of genre with the structure of argument employed. Surveying the existing economic literature, Massie observed that "Some Writers have considered Commerce as a Science, and endeavoured to deduce the Knowledge of it from Axioms, Maxims, &c., while many others have treated it as a Branch of History, and given Narratives of Transactions, Occurrences, &c." Most writers "have not considered Commerce either as a Science or as a Branch of History, but have mixed personal with national Affairs and blended Principles, History, and Practice together" (ii). How should the analysis of commerce proceed to produce true knowledge? Massie perceptively realized this was a question of textual genre.

8.5 The Link Between Prose Genres and Authoritative Reasoning

The various concerns about proper argument structure and rhetorical style expressed by late seventeenth and early eighteenth century writers on economic topics do not simply point to uncertainty about how such works should be classified. Through the psychological theory of mental faculties, prose genres were directly linked to modes of reasoning, so that affiliation with one category of textual discourse or another entailed claims to a specific kind epistemological and ontological legitimacy. In the second half of the eighteenth century, writers on economic topics increasingly began to employ conventions of discourse drawn from empiricist scientific methodology. Economic historians explain this as the coalescence of a common lexicon and analytic focus. Terence Hutchison, for example, writes, "By the middle of the century, certain fundamental general-theoretical questions regarding values and prices, and money and trade, with their ramifications and interdependencies, had come more clearly and explicitly into focus" (1988, 187). Writers who assumed a semi-autonomous realm of economic forces and institutions tended to incorporate a rudimentary circular flow model, in which the circulation of money determined prices and rates of interest, while self-adjusting processes regulated the quantity of money in circulation, price levels, and the volume of trade. The growing authority of such modes of discourse was not simply a consensus about core concepts and models, however, but also about the adoption of a specific narrative genre. Within this textual form, a certain type of representation was defined as evidence (examples drawn from the commercial world and numerical data), structure of argument (identifying a small number of principles capable of explaining diverse phenomena), and narrative style (unadorned and focused on explanation rather than persuasion).

The connection between the authority claimed by a particular type of economic reasoning and a distinct textual form becomes more apparent when we consider theories of prose genre developed in the eighteenth century. A number of Scottish Enlightenment writers composed treatises on rhetoric and belles letters that reworked traditional theories of discourse to incorporate the "new species of writing." George Campbell's *The Philosophy of Rhetoric* (c. 1750, p. 1776) undertook a scientific consideration of rhetoric and its relation to the different faculties of the mind. Whether composing oral or textual, scientific or persuasive discourses, the effective orator needed to "engage in his service all the different powers of the mind, the imagination, the memory, and the passions" (72). Since each mode of discourse targeted a particular cognitive function, each had a specific form of address. In defining the forms of composition appropriate to each faculty, Campbell identified rhetorical and structural elements proper to different genres of communication. Campbell did not, however, differentiate spoken and written forms of discourse. Adam Smith was the first develop a theory of prose compositions separate from oratory (Bradbury 2003, 42–45).

Being compiled from student notes, Smith's *Lectures on Rhetoric and Belles Lettres* is not as systematic in its treatment as Campbell's treatise. Eighteen of the lectures analyze various forms of discourse, both oral and written, and Smith intended to characterize the subject matter, structure, and rhetorical style of each. Presentational mode is used to categorize discourse as didactic (focused on instruction), narrative (focused on relaying facts), or rhetorical (focused on persuasion). Didactic writing includes philosophical works such as Virgil's *Georgics* and Shaftesbury's *An Inquiry Concerning Virtue or Merit*, as well as those in which "the Design is to Deliver a System of any Science," such as the natural philosophies of Aristotle and Newton (Smith 1985, 144). Smith identified the rhetorical style and compositional structure appropriate to the genre of scientific discourse. Didactic writers must adhere to a plain and perspicuous style, since "studying much to vary the expression leads one also frequently into a dungeon of metaphysical obscurity" (8). Scientific argument can take two forms, "either like Aristotle go over the Different branches in the order they happen to cast up to us, giving a principle commonly a new one for every phaenomenon; or in the manner of Sir Isaac Newton we may lay down certain principles known or proved in the beginning, from whence we account for the severall Phenomenon, connecting all together by the same Chain" (145–146). The latter is "undoubtedly the best in all matters of Science" (146).

In mapping out a system of relations between eighteenth-century discursive forms, Smith thus embedded the authority of scientific reasoning in the formal conventions of a certain textual genre. Looking at Smith's own textual practice in the *Wealth of Nations*, it is easy to see that he used the rhetorical style and structure he identified with scientific discourse. Smith employed a Newtonian analysis in which economic development is accounted for by the division of labor and the accumulation of capital. Charles Bazerman has also pointed out out that the third part of the *Wealth of Nations* fits the Newtonian model in being "an account of all economic history from the Smithian perspective, much in the same way the Newton's *Principia,* having set out the principles that move the universe, then gives particular accounts of all the local motions" (1993, 192). It is important to remember, though, that Smith's version of economic rationality was not definitive. In the same year that the *Wealth of Nations* appeared, James Steuart published his *Principles of Political Economy*, which employed a very different argument structure and style. Also in 1776, Josiah Tucker described his collection of tracts on commerce as approaching questions of trade from an a prioiri and moral perspective, then from arguments of "daily Experience and Observation" (21). Even in the last quarter of the eighteenth century, multiple kinds of economic reasoning competed for legitimacy.

8.6 Conclusion

In tracts and treatises written throughout the late seventeenth and eighteenth century, then, writers participated in the struggle for discursive authority encoded in debates about the nature of systematic analysis. They reflected on the relationship between textual form and claims to knowledge through discussion of their representational strategies and the uncertain generic status of their own works. And they advanced different models for the structure of argument, the kinds of evidence, and the uses of rhetoric appropriate to analysis of economic topics, all of which are markers of textual genre. Because they make little contribution to the development of concepts and analytic frameworks that compose the modern discipline of economics, these texts receive little attention from scholars. Yet, studying them can help us understand how a certain prose genre became the authoritative mode of textual discourse about money and commerce. In other words, by analyzing the changing textual forms of these works, we can see how economic rationality first took on its modern form.

Bibliography

Bacon, Francis. 1863. *Of the Dignity and Advancement of Learning. Vol. 8–9 of The Works of Francis Bacon*, ed. James Spedding, Robert Ellis, and Douglas Heath. Cambridge, MA: Riverside Press.

Bazerman, Charles. 1993. Money Talks: The Rhetorical Project of the Wealth of Nations. In *Economics and Language*, ed. Willie Henderson, Tony Dudley-Evans, and Roger Backhouse, 173–199. New York: Routledge.

Bradbury, Jill Marie. 2003. New Science and the New 'Species of Writing': Eighteenth-Century Prose Genres. *Eighteenth-Century Life*. 27(1): 28–51.

Brewer, Anthony, ed. 2001. *Richard Cantillon, Essay on the Nature of Commerce in General*. Trans. Henry Higgs. New Brunswick: Transaction Publishers.

Cary, John. 1717. *A Discourse on Trade*. London.

Chambers, Ephraim. 1738. *Cyclopaedia: Or, An Universal Dictionary of the Arts and Sciences*. 2nd edition. London.

Gervaise, Isaac. 1720. *The System or Theory of the Trade of the Whole World*. London.

Hull, Charles, ed. 1899. *The Economic Works of Sir William Petty*. Vol. 2. Cambridge, MA: Cambridge University Press.

Hutchison, Terence. 1988. *Before Adam Smith: The Emergence of Political Economy 1662–1776*. New York: Basil Blackwell.

Jones, R.F. 1951. *The Seventeenth Century: Studies in the History of English Thought and Literature from Bacon to Pope*. Palo Alto: Stanford University Press.

Knowlson, James. 1975. *Universal Language Schemes in England and France, 1600–1800*. Toronto: University of Toronto Press.

Locke, John. 1959. *An Essay Concerning Human Understanding*, ed. Alexander Campbell Fraser, Vol. 2. New York: Dover Publications.

Massie, Joseph. 1740. *Representation Concerning the Knowledge of Commerce as a National Concern*. London.

McCulloch, J.R., ed. 1954 (1856). *Early English Tracts on Commerce*. Cambridge, MA: Cambridge University Press.

McKeon, Michael. 1987. *The Origins of the English Novel, 1600–1740*. Baltimore: The Johns Hopkins University Press.

North, Dudley. 1691. *Discourses Upon Trade*. London.

Poovey, Mary. 1998. *A History of the Modern Fact: Problems of Knowledge in the Sciences of Wealth and Society*. Chicago: Johns Hopkins University Press.

Smith, Adam. 1985. *Lectures on Rhetoric and Belles Lettres*, ed. J.C. Bryce. Indianapolis: Liberty Fund.

Sprat, Thomas. 1958. *History of the Royal Society*, ed. Jackson Cope and Harold Whitmore Jones. St. Louis: Washington University Studies.

Stephens, James. 1972. Bacon's New English Rhetoric and the Debt to Aristotle. *Speech Monographs* 39: 248–259.

Chapter 9
Political Economy and Its Public Contenders 1820–1850

Stefan Gaarsmand Jacobsen and Thomas Palmelund Johansen

9.1 Introduction

From the 1820s to the 1840s, political economy was becoming established as a science in its own right (Augello and Guidi 2001), but the main doctrines to support this scientific development was questioned both by certain founding fathers and by those who challenged its universal applicability. The question of interest became central here: could political economists dress themselves in the ropes of the uninterested scientist searching only for observable natural laws? Or was there indeed a question of political interest to be tackled on every page of a treatise on political economy? In many aspects, the theoretical debates on interest and general applicability of economic ideas echoed the French and British writings on political economy emerging in the 1760s and 1770s. In this chapter, we want to highlight the ways in which claims to a scientific authority on the economy was constructed and attacked in both Britain and France. The main reason for investigating this case across the Channel, is that there was a common understanding that economic and social questions were not only applicable in one national setting. There was an awareness of the structural similarities in the industrial developments and in the different possible political responses (Prothero 2006). Thus, both the emerging group of self-professed "political economists" and their critics often related to debates and writings traveling between these two early movers of European industrialism. This chapter provides a comparative analysis of the two opposite notions of economic rationalities in a French and British context. In turn, these comparative insights will

S.G. Jacobsen (✉)
Department of Management, Politics and Philosophy, Copenhagen Business School, Frederiksberg, Denmark
e-mail: sgj.mpp@cbs.dk

T.P. Johansen
Department of Culture and Society, Aarhus University, Aarhus, Denmark
e-mail: tjohansen@cas.au.dk

J. Bek-Thomsen et al. (eds.), *History of Economic Rationalities*, Ethical Economy 54, DOI 10.1007/978-3-319-52815-1_9

allow us to end with a discussion of one of the first Modern European struggles over whether or not the economy should be regarded as a political object for scrutiny.

9.2 The Struggle to Establish a Political Science

Establishing a scientific discipline involves several key elements crucial in order to gain and maintain scientific authority. To name just a few, these are: foundation of clubs or learned societies; certain specialized channels of information and knowledge exchange such as correspondence network, periodical journals or scientific magazines; a professorship at the universities; a formalisation of methodology; a common subject to which it relates (Augello and Guidi 2001, 3ff; Stapelbroek and Marjanen 2012, 18–19). The important thing about these features is that they must be recognizable to the public in a way that makes the individual proponent of the new discipline stand out as representative of the science as a whole; or to rephrase: the discipline has to appear as unified field of investigation centered around the same object of inquiry.

This was exactly what the British writers in political economy attempted to achieve in the first decades of the nineteenth century. They struggled to give their discipline the same scientific authority as the natural sciences, and indeed this was a time when new disciplines emerged. The writings and correspondences of the political economists show signs of awareness among themselves of the importance of being recognised as one unified scientific discipline. In turn, as we shall see, the success of British political economists paved the way for French colleagues to claim that their liberal economic principles should be the backbone of any real "political science" in the 1830s and 1840s (Breton 1985, 236). Despite a number of differences in the content of British and French economic theories of this time, what was shared was the basic rationality of exclusively owning the theoretical keys that could solve the problems of modern industrial developments. These keys were dominated by a belief in free trade and a critique of any disturbances of market mechanisms by either governments or specific interest groups, like skilled labourers. At the height of the influence of the French liberal political economy, one of its leading proponents, Michel Chevalier, stated that "political economy is for the social body what physiology is to the human body" (Chevalier 1844, 17). The political economy was seen as *one* specific economic outlook with roots in the British tradition and that had been adapted and co-developed by Chevalier's mentor, Jean-Baptiste Say. As the great synthesizer between French and British economic thought, Say had published several editions of his *Traité d'économie politique* since 1803. After the fall of Napoleon, Say had been able to step up his rhetoric of imagining political economy as the answer to most political problems in Europe. From 1831 onwards, he was professor of political economy at the prestigious Collège de France, inspiring a new generation of liberal political economists, who shared the view that their economic principles gave rise to "the political science par excellence." Political economy, in this understanding, was the only science that could guarantee political liberty and the security of the people (Breton 1985).

In 1821, James Mill, Robert Malthus and a group of writers on political economy around them including Ricardo founded the Political Economy Club in London. This was seen, from both sides of the Channel, as an important step in the development of the science (Ricardo 2004a, 380–381; Say 2004, 36). In the original rules of the club it clearly states that all members should strive to spread the sound doctrines of the science. Most important in this context is the mentioning in the clubs statutes of the "duty of the Society, individually and collectively, to aid the circulation of all Publications [...] useful to the Science" (PEC1860, 24). The most esteemed man of science of the day, Cambridge philosopher William Whewell was perhaps one of the biggest critics of the classical political economist from within the established scientific community. Though a strong supporter of political economy, Whewell attacked Ricardo's and Mill's doctrines for not being sufficiently supported by empirical evidence. Whewell was actually ahead of his time in insisting on a much more extensive use of mathematics in political economy, and he was also a great influence alongside Charles Babbage in setting up the statistical section under the newly established *British Association of the Advancement of Science* (BAAS) in 1833. This made British political economy even more closely linked to Whig middle-class scientific culture, values and interests. The BAAS was to be the place for value free and purely objective science. Though Whewell insisted that men of science refrained themselves from political issues the political economists was usually not shy of making use of the expert knowledge in political discussions (Redman 1997, 93–99, 151–157; Morrell and Thackray 1981, 291–296).

One of the most telling expressions of the notion of the *interest* of political economy as a science is found within the private correspondences of political economist John R. McCulloch and his mentor David Ricardo. With the addition of a chapter "On Machinery" in the third edition of his *On the Principles of Political Economy and Taxation* (1821), Ricardo had changed his opinion on this subject, and now thought to provide evidence showing, in a scientifically deductive manner, that the introduction of machinery in manufacture was in fact not in the interest of all classes of society. Rather, Ricardo found, the use of machinery worked directly against the interest of the working classes by effectively reducing the wage fund (Ricardo 2004b, 386–397).

This change of mind was extremely disturbing to McCulloch. He regarded the new chapter as an immediate threat to the science. In McCulloch's eyes, the chapter represented: "a very material deduction from the value of the work" and was "doing a very serious injury to your favourite science" (McCulloch 2004, 382). To be sure, a scientist had the right to admit and correct errors in his theory, "but this may be done in various ways [...]" (McCulloch 2004, 382). Ricardo was reminded that:

> Your object never has been and never can be any other than to endeavour to promote the real interests of the science; but I apprehend you will agree with me in thinking that nothing can be more injurious to these interests than to see an Economist of the highest reputation strenuously defending one set of opinions one day, unconditionally surrendering them the next. (McCulloch 2004, 382)

The American economist Paul A. Samuelson has summarized the reaction of some of Ricardo's closest disciples with this caricature: "Even if it were true, don't publish it. Readers will only be confused. And why dilute the readers' admiration for *laissez faire*?" (Samuelson 1989, 49). This line of thought certainly seems adequate in the description of McCulloch's answer.

What is striking about McCulloch's harsh reaction is the extreme concern for public image of political economy, and we notice the reference to the "the interest of the science" that implies a notion of continuous progress within a clearly defined field of research. Furthermore McCulloch reflects on the absurdity of the fact that if Ricardo's view is right "[...] the laws against the Luddites are a disgrace to the Statute book" (McCulloch 2004, 385).

In response to the critique Ricardo writes a letter back stating that he had no fears whatsoever for reputation of the discipline just because he finally succeeded in drawing the right conclusions from his fundamental doctrines: "I cannot agree with you that it will arm those, who have contended that Political Economy is a fabric without a foundation, with any additional arguments in favor [sic] of that opinion" (Ricardo 2004c, 387). Whether Ricardos chapter added fuel to the critics' fire or not is hard to determine within the scope of this current chapter, however the correspondence clearly shows that importance and indeed the difficulties of trying to appear as one unified discipline. Indeed, a decade and a half later James Mill found it necessary to defend the notion of a unified scientific discipline with a firm foundation and distinct object when he wrote the dialogue "Whether Political Economy is Useful?" in the *Westminster Review* (Mill 1836).

9.3 British Critique

In post-Napoleonic Britain of the 1820s and 1830s, radical critique of the classical political economist and their heirs among the political elite might at first sight seem rather ambiguous. On the one hand, their writings indicated a growing anti-intellectual attitude when complaining that the economists too readily put every aspect of human life on the same line of the equation. We find this concern against scientific reductivism expressed by other sceptics as well, e.g. Charles Dickens and Tory writers such as the Samuel Taylor Coleridge and Robert Southey (Eastwood 2004). On the other hand, we also find among the radical critics a strong emphasis on "true" science, "real" truth, and "really" useful knowledge.

In 1832 the public debates about economics was not merely centered around the words of the higher level of economists, but also around the works of the popularizers of political economy to a broader audience. In the centre of it all stood *The Society for the Diffusion of Useful Knowledge* (SDUK), a philanthropic society established by Henry Brougham and James Mill, among others, with the purpose of spreading sound and scientific knowledge among the labouring classes as an antidote to the radical agitators' unstamped papers. The SDUK was widely referred to in the radical press as a metonymy for a Whig capitalist class representing malthusian middle-class ideology in its purest form. Commenting on a recent publication on machinery the leading unstamped paper *The Poor Man's Guardian* assessed that the object of the SDUK was:

> to cause the few to take from the millions the whole produce of their labour; and to accomplish this object, they endeavour, by all sorts of sophistry, to delude wealth producers into a belief that the labour of human beings is regulated precisely upon the same principles as any other commodity. (*Poor Man's Guardian, Jan 7,* 1832, 236)

The message here is quite clear: The political economists, speaking through the medium of the SDUK's self-proclaimed scientific treatises, expressed nothing but the interests of the capitalist class. Quoting from the SDUK big seller *Results of Machinery* (1831) as if it was a catalogue of malthusian prejudices, the *Guardian* attacked the classical political economist building on malthusian doctrines of individualist battle for survival in the competitive industrialized society: "The juggle of the political economists, [...], is now seen through; when translated into English, political economy means nothing more nor less than this – Give up the whole produce of your labour – fill everybody's cupboard but your own – and then starve quietly ! ! !" (*Poor Man's Guardian, Jan 7,* 1832, 237). During the third Co-operative Congress in London, held in late April, 1,832, the SDUK again had to take the fire several times for their inappropriate remedies to the problems of overpopulation and general glut. The SDUK were ridiculed for not realising that these problems were systemic and stemmed from the errors of the current government (See e.g. Carpenter 1832, 8 and 21ff). The present government was ascribed a strong belief in the principle of competition as the "principle upon which government depended" and through the medium such as the SDUK they had "taught mankind to compete with each other, and to outstrip his brother by every means in his power" (Reported in *Poor Man's Guardian, May 5*, 1832, 379).

Though Ricardo's influence on the socialist and Chartist writers is well known, it is evident that they especially loathed the classical political economist, and many shared the wish of William Cobbett that "the Scotch political economy is blown to the devil, and the Edinburgh Review and Adam Smith along with it" (Cobbett 1830, 458; see also Thompson 1984). A central target was the Whig embracement of Malthus's theory of population and Ricardo's and McCulloch's political economy, combined with the disciplining attempts of middle-class industrialists and Whig social reformers such as Henry Brougham and Harriet Martineau to replace the supposed "sensual" lifestyle with a rational behavior in accordance with the doctrines of political economy as well as Christian morals (Huzel 2006, 41, 163–231; Firth 2005). To be sure, it was not the idea that there existed such a thing as *the* economy, guided by certain natural law and determining the distribution of wealth in society that was being questioned. Rather, the problem was the privilege of the middle-class writers in political economy to monopolise the readings of the grand book of wealth in accordance to their own interests. As ricardian socialist writer and public lecturer on the subject, Thomas Hodgskin, proclaimed:

> Political economy is natural science, not a political science, and must not be left exclusively to statesmen. It originated among practical men and it does not end in barren speculation

> [...] we cannot acknowledge, therefore, that we are incapable of ascertaining and understanding the natural laws which regulates the progress of society, without giving into the hands of one class of men the power of interpreting them according to their own views and interest. (Hodgskin 1827, 263)

Hodgskin contrasted the practical men concerned with the practical arrangement of society with speculating venture capitalists concerned only with their own potential gain, and not seeing the risk they might impose on people less resilient to economic loss. Indeed, for socialist reformer Robert Owen and his weekly unstamped paper *The Crisis*, the comparison to priestcraft was almost too tempting not to draw: "Except Church polemics, there is no class of men so given to verbosity – so guilty of perpetrating quarto after quarto and of taking infinite pains to conceal the small needle of simple truth in the great straw-bottle of elaborate argument – as the Political Economist" (Owen and Owen 1832, 107).

One way of making sense of the mixed critique made by the radical artisans of their middle-class antagonists as being scientistic and at the same time non-scientific is by keeping in mind the broader cultural context in which science played a key role. It is well established that in the beginning of nineteenth century Britain science served as a focal point in the building of a progressivist middle-class culture and thus as social legitimation of socially ambitious manufacturers seeking social control and political influence (Thackray 1974; Barnes and Shapin 1977). But science was also an important part of working-class culture in the 1820s and 1830s. In fact scientific counter cultures can be traced among artisans in the period in direct opposition to the middle- and upper-class "gentlemen of science" (Desmond 1989; Secord 1994; for Gentlemen of science: Morrell and Thackray 1981). There were attempts within radical parts of the working classes to create a genuine working-class science, and it is useful to see the rejection of the classical political economist in this light. Adrian Desmond has argued in his seminal work on *The Politics of Evolution* (1989), that anti-malthusianism and the critique of "the spirit of competition" was often coupled with a strong Lamarckian vision of society progressing through cooperation (see also Hale 2014). Malthus had re-introduced the old problem of human sociability and self-interest in the bodily language of reproduction. A radical social reading of Lamarck's theory of biological transmutation placed a genuine opportunity for political change from below within nature itself. Instead of the books and magazine of the would-be middle-class educators, meant for "rational recreation," there was a call for mutual working-class education that would work as a leverage for the evolutionary progress of labouring orders. The working-class political economy which was developed in the pages of the radical papers (See esp. Thompson 1984) might therefore be seen as part of a larger pattern of counter scientific discourse, and hence represent a specific working-class economic rationality, at least in the name of the self-proclaimed spokesmen of the labouring classes.

9.4 French Critique

French developments from the 1830s provide a useful comparison to the British case. Although French industries were not as advanced as British counterparts, certain trades had the industrial capacity to form the background for debate on political economy. Silk weaving, one of the most advanced industries in France at this time, involved a lot of skilled workers, the so-called Canutes, under the auspices of successful fabricants. The first successful French newspaper to explicitly claimed to be an organ of the workers – the *Echo de la Fabrique* – was founded in 1831 (Frobert 2010).

Under French censorship, the *Echo* officially had to be non-political and was therefore not able to report about ongoing political initiatives of the workers. In turn, the writings about workers' conditions became directed at the question of political economy and more abstract debates regarding the mechanization of industry (Popkin 2002, 34). This paved the way for a criticism of the proclaimed sciences of political economy, in which several doctrines were seen as harmful to the workers and, subsequently, a demand for a rethinking of economic theories to accommodate the political situation.

The political environment of 1830s France was somewhat more tumultuous than the British, the French "liberal revolution" of 1830 becoming a changing point for the view of economic liberalism vis-a-vis the worker's rights. This was especially the case in Lyon, the city in which some of the harshest uprisings against economic policies took place among the silk weavers. The leaders of Lyon had established a "society of mutual duty" that could effectively organize strikes in a position to either governmental policies that would shrink their salaries or the conditions on specific factories (Sheridan 1979, 218). The success of this society led to its prohibition by central government in Paris after several attempts of organizing general strike among all members in 1834. The result was a deep difference in understanding of what the government program of promoting free enterprise would mean for members of society.

For the radical artisans and workers, free enterprise came to mean the freedom of the merchants and fabricants to exploit an unorganized workforce rather than to promote freedom in all areas of human activity, including the right to form societies. Upon looking back at his experiences, in 1848 master weaver Vernay deemed it to be "a truth known well by all honest men, that unlimited freedom of trade is a license favoring devious and greedy men" (Quoted in Sheridan 1979, 219). This development was mirrored in the innovative press of the working classes in the 1830s. Here, we can identify another layer of the criticism of economic liberalism, namely that of the scientistic nature of the theories viewed as instructive for government policies and, in turn, inhibited for the improvement of labor's livelihood.

One of the most important questions not being debated in the echo was the question of salaries for the French silk workers of Lyon. For the leading writers of the *Echo*, this was a topic that brought up the hypocrisy of the political elites and signs of scientism of the French classical economists of the day. Antoine Vidal, writer, tulle worker and school teacher (Popkin, 142), interpreted the standard sentiments among the higher classes and contrasted it with the interest of the workers:

> Everyone knows that the workers cannot live [off his salaries], and that we must seek ways to alleviate the condition of this class, which is too large to be neglected. Everyone thinks they find the infallible remedy without realizing that they argue in their own interest, and that it is a logic, which can be explained in a few simple words: I want the worker to become happy, but it cannot cost me anything (*Echo de la Fabrique*, 25 décembre 1831 – Numéro 9).

Vidal identified this flawed moral stance as a specific logic that proved itself especially problematic in a situation in which the workers were able to communicate specific demands. Leaving objections to this logic unspoken would "allow the trader to evade any talk of increased wages" and uphold a benevolent face whilst expecting government to "alleviate all the burdens of the poor class." Importantly, the role of the tradesmen and factory owners is not to produce this logic, merely to take advantage of it. This is where the critique of political economists come to the fore. The lack of understanding of the workers' problems stems from "Always sophistry and nothing but sophistry! we return constantly to the talk of taking away from the worker, but not one of these philanthropists, these economists says that he [the worker] should be given more."

The sarcasm over the philanthropy and scientific approach was aimed at the promises of an economic system that would benefit all groups and classes of the French society. For the editors of the *Echo*, this was seen as a reflex of the most orthodox economic theory of the day. The republican poet Dufaitelle wrote that

> Today, all of France, and especially the home of M. Say, the city of Lyon, attacks the system of free competition, and reverts to French ideas of organization and direction. It is our duty to help this trend as much as possible in our humble sphere of activity (*Echo*, 9 novembre 1834 – Numéro 8)

According to Dufaitelle, Say had been too heavily influenced by the "British school," making him too certain of the "universality of political economy." The resulting endorsement of a system of free competition was seen as being both a possible path for actual policies and a theoretical approach. For Dufaitelle, to "revert to French ideas" would mean to counter Say by taking into account the normative approach of Charles Fourier – known for his socialist experiments with shared property:

> The trader is a ruinous intermediary between the producer and the consumer. He exploits both. Mr. Fourier gave a very sharp and very true definition of commerce: according to him, it is the art of buying for three francs that which is worth six, and selling for six francs that which is worth three (ibid.).

The critique thus rhetorically connected the attack on the traders of Lyon with an attack on the understanding of value entailed by classical political economy. While Dufaitelle's approach to the relation between price and value seems reconcilable with classical political economy's labor theory of value, it implied that too naïve an endorsement of free trade could lead to the dominance of "players" of the market. Indeed, in what has since been called "Say's law," the merchant was explicitly not counted. For Say there was no "ruinous intermediary" between producers and consumers:

> As each of us can only purchase the productions of others with his own productions – as the value we can buy is equal to the value we can produce, the more men can produce, the more they will purchase. (Say 1834, 3)

It was this overoptimistic approach to market exchanges that made Dufaitelle and other writers of the *Echo* react to classical political economy.

Interestingly, the critique found in the *Echo* was partially shared by Say's successor as the professor of political economy at Collège de France, Adolphe Blanqui. Although fundamentally a supporter of Say's free trade principles, Blanqui had at least two other major influences: The doctrines of the so-called saint-simonians and the revolutionary socialist movement of which his brother, Auguste Blanqui, was part. Adolphe Blanqui urged his fellow political economists to "Respect the utopians [Socialists] who accuse you of carelessness and blush at their minor mistakes because they sacrifice their lives for millions of ungrateful people" (Blanqui in Breton 1986, 241). Unlike his brother, Adolphe Blanqui was not a socialist, but he was very aware of the dangers in the attempt to apply too simple utilitarian principles of the "British school" to the human rights orientated post-revolutionary French debate on economic justice (Sigot 2010).

Henri Saint-Simon had engaged in broad theorisations on how to place science as a driving industrial and religious force in society. However, after his death a small group of economically interested disciples focused on Saint-Simon's ideas on production as an alternative to the liberalism of Say and his followers. Saint-Simon had applied the term "industrialism" for his approach to the economy that emphasized scientific expertise and engineering as holding the keys to economic development. After his death in 1825, it was saint-simonians who invented the term "socialism" as they began to include class-interest in their economic theories (Olson 2008, 53). As in the case of Adolphe Blanqui, it was therefore possible for economic thinkers to intermix different rationalities at play in this period.

However, gradually the many possible philosophical, practical and political systems at play became a conflictual topic. As the socialist movements became even more class-oriented, Joseph Garnier, a critical voice from the camp of liberal political economy argued that the lack of epistemological clarity was the main problem of the socialists:

> They [the Socialists] have tried to orientate themselves in the midst of many systems that are often quite opposite to each other: the Saint-Simonianism, Fourierism, Owenism, Communism [...]. (Garnier 1843, 11)

The reference to both French and British systems testify to the awareness of border-crossing inspirations for the socialist movements. Although the critique of political economy coming from the emerging working class literature had struck a chord with French intellectuals in the 1830s, the support was disappearing as the transnational clash between political economy and socialism was intensifying in the 1840s (Breton 1985, 242).

9.5 Rationalities, Interests and Competing Sciences

French liberals accepted the socialist ideas as long as it was kept to basic economic questions that had been at the core of the *Echo*: how the individual worker should secure his own "just" salary and how proper working conditions were upheld. However, if the socialists began to claim that they had a science of their own that could serve as a basis for specific government action, the liberals were on the attack. In other words, when the socialist rationalities became the backbone of a complete vision for changing society, it went too strongly against the liberal economic creed. After the popularity of radical socialist ideas had become evident in the 1848 revolution, liberal writers such as Frederic Bastiat, Gustave de Molianari specifically targeted socialism as "alchemical" or the equivalent of "astrology" against the "astronomy" of political economy (Bastiat 1849; Molinari 1849). The political rationality of the socialists were pitted as unscientific as opposed to the liberal basic notions of rationality, which was supposed to stand comparison with any natural science. Sociologist of science Thomas F. Gieryn has described this demarcation of science as non-science as "boundary-work" (Gieryn 1983). The structure of this argument did not rid, however, the liberal economists of political enemies in France. The conservatives, with their landed interests, remained equally problematic for the French liberals and were also to be kept from power. The question of interest was central in both regards, whether it being the interest of the least affluent or the most in society who could build up intentions to apply political control of the economy.

As opposed to these French developments, British political economists had succeeded in winning the conservative party over to their side on the question of (international) free trade during the 1840s with the repeal of the corn laws in 1846 as an important turning point (Eastwood 2004). Similarly, the British radical workers had increasingly come under the guidance of classical political economy after the Chartist movement started weakening in the 1840s, gradually accepting fluctuations in their salaries as a legitimate and law-like economic pattern (Host 1998, 35; Prothero 2006, 136). Vice versa, socialist ideas had an impact on classical economy. In the approach of John Stuart Mill, which became "textbook" after his *Principles* in 1848, socialism was not to be trusted as a system, but still contained ideas that could serve as an inspiration. Mill's openness to consider the benevolence of cooperatives and workers' ownership of enterprises testify to the fact that he sought a dialogue with socialists rather than to crush them (Hamburger 2001, 144). This differentiation between moral and scientific principles worked as an argument against a more comprehensive version of socialist or popular political economy.

Despite the differences in political trajectories and influence of liberal political economists in France and Britain, the allusion to science and rationalities as weapons against socialist economic theories was quite similar. This is not surprising in light of the mentioned strengthening of the political and ideational ties among political economists on both sides of the channel in the first half of the nineteenth century. Apart from the development of similar theories, the strategy involved in using the suppressing socialist critics seems also to have been an area of mutual inspiration.

9.6 Concluding Remarks

In 1888, looking back upon the revolutionary moment of 1848, Friedrich Engels wrote that "socialism was, in 1847, a middle-class movement, communism a working-class movement. Socialism was, on the Continent at least, "respectable;" communism was the very opposite" (Engels 2012 [1888], 85). For Engels, this served as a reason why he and Marx opted for the communist rather than the socialist manifesto as the title of their pamphlet – it marked it clear that economic rationalities were *political* and not simply part of the arena of an interest-free science that political economists had lured the socialists into. As we have seen, the journals and newspapers of radical artisans in England and France had given voice to a lot of skepticism vis-a-vis the established notions of political economy. The outcome, however, was more of an adjustment of liberal political economy than the emergence of a new science of the economy that was primarily directed at bettering the conditions of the working classes. This intermixing between different economic rationalities and claims to scientificness is part of the background for the Marxist ambition of creating knowledge about the economy that was both political and scientific. More generally, this intermixing marked the beginning of the ongoing debate on what constitutes the most scientific approach to economic realities. A debate that continues in today's clash between orthodox and heterodox economics, in which the specialization of publication channels has put an end to the intermixing of ideas, but not to the question itself.

Bibliography

Augello, M.M., and M.E. Guidi. 2001. *The Spread of Political Economy and the Professionalisation of Economists: Economic Societies in Europe, America and Japan in the Nineteenth Century.* London/New York: Routledge.

Barnes, B., and S. Shapin. 1977. Science, Nature and Control: Interpreting Mechanics' Institutetes. *Social Studies in Science* 7(1): 31–74.

Bastiat, Frédéric. 1849. Disarmament and Taxes. In *French Liberalism in the 19th Century*, eds. Robert Leroux and, David Hart, 2012. London: Routledge.

Breton, Yves. 1985. Les économistes, le pouvoir politique et l'ordre social en France en 1830 et 1851. *Histoire, économie et société* 4(2): 233–252.

Carpenter, William. 1832. *Proceedings of the Third Co-operative Congress: Held in London, and Composed of Delegates of Co-Operative Societies of Great Britain and Ireland.* London: William Strange.

Chevalier, M. 1844. *Annuaire de l'économie politique pour 1844, 1re année: agriculture, industrie, commerce.* Paris: Guillaumin.

Cobbett, William. 1830. *Rural Rides.* London: Cobbett.

Desmond, Adrian. 1989. *The Politics of Evolution: Morphology, Medicine, and Reform in Radical London.* Chicago: The University of Chicago Press.

Eastwood, D. 2004. Tories and Markets: Britain 1800–1850. In *Markets in Historical Contexts: Ideas and Politics in the Modern World*, ed. M. Bevir and F. Trentmann. Cambridge, MA/New York: Cambridge University Press.

Engels, Friedrich. 2012 [1888]. Preface to the English Edition. In *The Communist Manifesto: A Modern Edition*, ed. K. Marx and F. Engels. London: Verso.

Firth, Ann. 2005. Culture and Wealth Creation: Mechanics' Institutes and the Emergence of Political Economy in Early Nineteenth-Century Britain. *History of Intellectual Culture* 5(1): 1–14.

Frobert, L. 2010. *L'Écho de la fabrique naissance de la presse ouvrière à Lyon, 1831–1834*. Lyon: ENS Éd.

Frobert, L. et al. ed. 2016. *Echo de la fabrique*. http://echo-fabrique.ens-lyon.fr/. Accessed 25 Nov 2016.

Garnier, J. 1843. *Ouverture du Cours d'économie politique à l'Athénée royal, juin 1843*. Paris.

Gieryn, Thomas F. 1983. Boundary-Work and the Demarcation of Science from Non-Science: Strains and Interests in Professional Ideologies of Scientists. *American Sociological Review* 48(6): 781–795.

Hale, Peirs J. 2014. *Political Descent: Malthus, Mutualism, and the Politics of Evolution in Victorian England*. Chicago/London: The University of Chicago Press.

Hamburger, J. 2001. *John Stuart Mill on Liberty and Control*. Princeton: Princeton University Press.

Hodgskin, Thomas. 1827. *Popular Political Economy. Four Lectures Delivered at the London Mechanics Institution*. London: Charles and William Tait.

Host, John. 1998. *Victorian Labour History: Experience, Identity and the Politics of Representation*. London: Routhledge.

Huzel, James P. 2006. *The Popularization of Malthus in Early Nineteenth-Centry England: Martineau, Cobbett and the Pauper Press*. Aldershot: Ashgate Publishing Limited.

McCulloch, John Ramsay. 2004. McCulloch to Ricardo, Edinburg 5. June 1821. In *The Works and Corresponces of David Ricardo*, ed. P. Sraffa, Vol. 8, 381–386. Indianapolis: Liberty Fund.

Mill, James. 1836, January. Whether Political Economy is Useful?. *Westminster Review* 2(4): 553–571. London: J. Macrone.

Molinari, Gustave 1849. The private production of Security In *French Liberalism in the 19th Century*, eds. Leroux, Robert and David Hart. 2012. London: Routledge.

Morrell, J., and A. Thackray. 1981. *Gentlemen of Science: British Association for the Advancement of Science*. Oxford: Clarendon.

Olson, R. 2008. *Science and Scientism in Nineteenth-Century Europe*. Urbana: University of Illinois Press.

Owen, R., and R.D. Owen, ed. 1832. *The Crisis, Or The Change from Error and Misery to Truth and Happiness*. Vol. 1. London: J. Eamonson.

PEC, Political Economy Club. 1860. *Political Economy Club, Founded in London, 1821. Names of Members 1821–1860: – Rules of the Club: – and List of Questions Discussed 1833–1860*. London: Printed for the Club.

Popkin, J.D. 2002. *Press, Revolution, and Social Identities in France, 1830–1835*. University Park: Pennsylvania State University Press.

Prothero, I.J. 2006. *Radical Artisans in England and France, 1830–1870*. Cambridge, MA: Cambridge University Press.

Redman, Deborah A. 1997. *The Rise of Political Economy as a Science: Methodology and the Classical Economists*. Cambridge, MA: MIT Press.

Ricardo, David. 2004a. Ricardo to Say, 8 May 1821. In *The Works and Correspondences of David Ricardo*, ed. P. Sraffa, Vol. 8, 379–381. Indianapolis: Liberty Fund.

———. 2004b. *On the Principles of Political Economy and Taxation, 3rd Edition*. In *The Works and Correspondences of David Ricardo*, Vol. 1, ed. Sraffa, P. Indianapolis: Liberty Fund.

———. 2004c. Ricardo to McCulloch, London 18. June 1821. In *The Works and Correspondences of David Ricardo*, ed. P. Sraffa, Vol. 1, 386–391. Indianapolis: Liberty Fund.

Samuelson, Paul A. 1989. Ridardo Was Right! *The Scandinavian Journal of Economics* 91(1): 46–62.

Say, Jean-Baptiste. 1834. *A Treatise on Political Economy, Or, The Production, Distribution, and Consumption of Wealth*. Philadelphia: Grigg & Elliot.

———. 2004. Say to Ricardo, 19 July 1821. In *The Works and Correspondences of David Ricardo*, ed. P. Sraffa, Vol. 1, 31–36. Indianapolis: Liberty Fund.

Secord, Anne. 1994. Science in the Pub: Artisan Botanists in Early Nineteenth-century Lancashire. *History of Science* 32(3): 269–315.

Sheridan, G. 1979. The Political Economy of Artisan Industry: Government and the People in the Silk Trade of Lyon, 1830–1870. *French Historical Studies* 11(2): 215–238.

Sigot, Nathalie. 2010. Utility and Justice: French Liberal Economists in the 19th Century. *European Journal of the History of Economic Thought* 17: 759–792.

Stapelbroek, Koen, and Jani Marjanen. 2012. *The Rise of Economic Societies in the Eighteenth Century: Patriotic Reform in Europe and North America*. Basingstoke: Palgrave Macmillan.

Thackray, Arnold. 1974. Natural Knowledge in Cultural Context: The Manchester Mode. *The American Historical Review* 79(3): 672–709.

The Poor Man's Guardian Vol. 2 (1832). London: Henry Hetherington.

Thompson, Noel W. 1984. *The People's Science: The Popular Political Economy of Exploitation and Crisis 1816–1834*. Cambridge, MA: Cambridge University Press.

Chapter 10
The Promissory Self – Credit and Debt Rationalities in the Work and Life of Karl Marx

Mikkel Thorup

Credit and debit lead different lives. While being on the one hand mirror images of each other they operate with different rationalities, evoke different images and install different moralities. Credit is the loan when borrowing and it is filled with images and emotions of opportunity, freedom, past good behavior and future consumption as well as positive self-images centered round the notion of credibility. Debt is the loan when repaying and it is filled with horrifying images of constraint, obligations, sacrifice, past consumption and foregoing of future enjoyment centered also round the notion of credibility, but one now precarious and dependent upon steady repayments and other performances of credibility.

Credit and debt rationalities work because they invoke both an economic rationality of monetary repayment and contractual obligations as well as a moral rationality of trustworthiness and moral obligations. A "payback morality" exist which draws on parallel economic and moral ideas of obligations and on the self-imagery of the "promissory person," the one who can promise now what will be honored tomorrow, the one who can calculate one's present and future conditions and act accordingly, the one whose promissory notes turn into self-imagery. This intertwined relation between economic and moral rationalities is clearly evident in the way credit and debt act upon the individual, the way credit and debt is a subjectivizing force creating the subject fit to borrow. In the following I want to put body and motion into the promissory person by discussing two instances of Karl Marx's life and work, two instances where he at one time, in 1844 theorizes what I have termed the promissory person, and the second, in 1858, where he lives the life of one.

Credit, Karl Marx writes, is "the *economic* judgment on the *morality* of a man" (Marx 1844). Possibly more than any other economic issue, debt reveals the interrelations between economic and moral rationalities. There is a counting of balances, projections of the future, a commandment of payback and some not easily untangled

M. Thorup (✉)
Institute for Culture and Society, Aarhus University, Aarhus, Denmark
e-mail: idemt@cas.au.dk

J. Bek-Thomsen et al. (eds.), *History of Economic Rationalities*, Ethical Economy 54, DOI 10.1007/978-3-319-52815-1_10

relations between the economic and the moral in the notion of credit, of being credit worthy, of being of good credit. To be creditable is a specific way of being, of exhibiting being, and of being believed as such a being. It is, to paraphrase Marx, an economic, even when not spoken in economic terms, way of measuring someone's worth as a person and a debtor. In the debt relation "the *man* himself [sic], instead of metal and paper, has become the *mediator* of exchange, not however as a man, but as the *mode of existence of capital* and interest" (ibid.).

The debtor is positioned in a certain way socially and positions oneself too. There is a show of credibility in any borrower/debtor-relation and there are pronounced albeit often hidden moral issues at work in any economic credit situation. In this chapter I want to discuss how economic and moral rationalities interact, and I shall do so through the writings of Marx. But rather than focusing on his theoretical writings on credit in *Das Kapital* (especially book 3.4–5). I want to discuss two marginal texts related to what we could term the debt experience. The first text is from the Paris manuscript which Marx wrote from end of 1843 to the beginning of 1845 as a series of notes to books he read. The second is a letter from Marx to Friedrich Engels dated July 15, 1858. There are no overt links or references between the two texts but they do share some common features. They are private texts, notes and a letter, and they both grasp with the same moral issues of private indebtedness. In the notes there's a theoretical and in the letter a personal engagement with debt as a social relation and as a process and project of the self.

In his recent *The Making of the Indebted Man*, Maurizio Lazzarato enlists Marx' reading of Mill (as well as Nietzsche, Deleuze/Guattari and Foucault) in his contemporary critique of indebtedness as part of a neoliberal subjectivation (Lazzarato 2012). While I have no issues with that analysis my aim in reading the same text is another, namely the more general issue of how debt is always already overdetermined by not only its economic, calculable and payable issues, but also with moral issues of settling scores, paying one's dues and performing in all its dimensions what we refer to as a "payback morality."

10.1 A "Good" Man

In the beginning of the 1840s Marx was in Paris immersed in reading and writing. In the so-called Paris Manuscripts he wrote comments and excerpts from books he read. One of these books was James Mill's *Elements of Political Economy* published in 1821. Marx read a French translation and among his notes on Mill's book are some on debt, not least on debt as a social relation mediated not only through money and contracts but also through appearances and make believe. In the credit system it seems that the increasingly abstract currency (from objects to gold to paper) is reversed and that man is once again relating not to abstracts but to other people. Unlike capital, which exploits people and human labor for profit, credit seems to reinstall an interpersonal relation. But, Marx writes, this only established a new divide among people which is even more intrusive and fatal than the capital/work-relation.

The core of the debt relation is not money or the loan but a special interaction between creditor and debtor in which the creditor through the loan decision passes judgment on the loan seeker as a "good man" or not. The moral assumption of "good" is translatable to "a man who is 'able to pay'" (Marx 1844), or rather, Marx should have added, who shows himself "willing to pay." He mentions Shylock from William Shakespeare's *Merchant from Venice* where the money lender Shylock calls the borrower Antonio a good man, not because he is a moral man in a conventional sense – he and Shylock are commercial, religious and personal enemies – but because he is creditworthy. The duality between able and willing is probably more important than Marx realizes because the ability to pay concerns the outward possessions and relations of the potential borrower whereas the question of being willing to pay is where the soul and innermost being of the borrower is examined. This examination of the moral worth of the borrower is not only performed by the creditor but is a description the borrower applies to himself. The borrower does not only have debt as something external but is in deb. The borrower is a debtor, a certain way of being. He or she is not only a borrower but a debt person, defined and circumscribed by the pecuniary and moral implications of the loan.

Marx put forward two debt scenarios exposing the inequalities inherent in the debt relation. In the first "a rich man gives credit to a poor man whom he considers industrious and decent." This is an exception, a kind of romantic or maybe even feudal-paternalistic residue uncommon in capitalist societies. But, once that loan is given, "the life of the poor man and his talents and activity serve the rich man as a *guarantee* of the repayment of the money lent." The implication of this is "that all the social virtues of the poor man, the content of his vital activity, his existence itself, represent for the rich man the reimbursement of his capital with the customary interest" (ibid.). The entire being of the poor man is inscribed in the debt relation, made apparent for the creditor as part of his or her calculation. The second debt and to Marx more common scenario is when a loan is given to someone who already has means. Marx implies the system of enforcement in place here is not as stringent as in the first scenario where the creditor has "besides *moral* guarantees, also the guarantee of *legal* compulsion and still other more or less *real* guarantees" (ibid.). As stated above the debt relation depends upon trust but operates on distrust. Similarly, the debt relation like any exchange operates on the initial assumption of equality and acknowledgment. A loan contract is only possible when both parties acknowledge the other as someone able to enter into a contract. But at the same time the debt relation is dependent upon and reinforces an inequality where "man himself is turned into *money*, or money is *incorporated* in him" (ibid.), while he is having the moral character summarized numerically in the interest rate of the loan. In both scenarios, disregarding the different inequalities at work, "*human individuality*, human *morality* itself, has become both an object of commerce and the material in which money exists. Instead of money, or paper, it is my own personal existence, my flesh and blood, my social virtue and importance, which constitutes the material, corporeal form of the *spirit of money*" (ibid.). It is not really, Marx seems to argue, an interaction of economic and moral rationalities but the substitution of the moral and the human by the economic, or rather: the moral and the human is evaluated, made active and perceivable through the calculation of monetary worth.

The credit system has, Marx says, a tendency to maintain and deepen social inequality because "credit is given only to him who already has, and is a new opportunity of accumulation for the rich man" and because the poor "finds that the arbitrary discretion of the rich man and latter's judgment over him confirm or deny his *entire* existence and that his existence is wholly dependent on this contingency" (ibid.). Here one has to both confirm and transcend Marx. It seems obviously true that credit is mostly given to those who already have (if nothing else something alienable as collateral) and who use the loan to amass more. In Marx's time this was mainly business investment. Today we have to add investment in private consumption of an ever-increasing variety in what is increasingly termed "the financialization of daily life" (Martin 2002; Langley 2008). And we must notice the expansion of the circle of borrowers through installment credit, credit cards, microcredit etc. to just about everyone (Calder 1999; Kamenetz 2007). Still, we must maintain Marx's insight on the exposure of "the poor," only just no longer barred of credit, to the arbitrary judgment of the "rich," only now in the shape of the bank. So, Marx's thoughts on the debt relation between the "poor" and the "rich" must be maintained and supplemented; maintained because inequality is still a manifest economic and social reality and its incarnations in debt situations are no less strong now than then; but supplemented because Marx understood the "rich" as the one who could borrow money and the "poor" as the one excluded from the credit system, except for the occasional "benevolent" rich man. Today, most are "rich" in the sense of having access to some credit, although under highly unequal terms and prices, but at the same time also "poor" because the borrowing exposes us to an economic evaluation of our moral habitus. The economic evaluation of our credibility has become generalized as credit has expanded to cover the near totality of the social.

Credit is trust and acknowledgment as a "good person" but as I quoted Marx earlier, credit is also distrust and suspicion. About the person who is not creditworthy "is pronounced not only the simple judgment that he is poor, but in addition a pejorative moral judgment that he possesses no trust, no recognition, and therefore is a social pariah, a bad man" (ibid). The ultimate humiliation for the poor is having to ask the rich for credit and let an outsider "spying into the secrets of the private life" (ibid.). Trust is examined and calculated. Creditor and borrower perform a trust game where they both talk trust but act distrustful of the other. The debt relation depends on the trustworthiness the borrower demonstrates and the creditor acknowledges. But, Marx says, this trust relation manifests itself as distrust because every loan application is evaluated and priced according to the risk of default. The debt relation "is all the more *infamous* and *extreme* because its element is no longer commodity, metal, paper, but man's *moral* existence, man's *social* existence, the *inmost depths* of his heart, and because under the appearance of man's *trust* in man it is the height of *distrust* and complete estrangement" (ibid.). An inequality resides inside the debt relation, where the one, the borrower, must allow him- or herself to be made transparent, the innermost being, thoughts and inclinations exposed, and where every outer and inner expression is read as signs to be interpreted by the creditor. How is the borrower to act honestly when his or her moral stature is under examination? How is the creditor to trust anyone, knowing that the borrower too recognizes this as an examination? Signs read, signs displayed, invite distrust on both parts. The borrower resents the questioning of character and the creditor mistrusts the answer given. Espionage is the method of the creditor just as counterfeiting is that of the borrower. The latter has to arrange the facts of his or her life to appear "good," active, diligent, today we would add entrepreneurial. "*Counterfeiting*", Marx writes, "cannot be undertaken by man in any other material than his own person." The borrower "has to make himself into counterfeit coin" (ibid.), that is, appear as monetary value, take on the form of money, make him- or herself capital. The true horror of debt for Marx, it would appear, is that the monetarization goes deeper, turns intimate and personal, while the debtor has to estrange him- or herself from human worth and personal character in order to appear and act the monetary part.

10.2 Letter to a Friend

While the Paris Manuscripts were a theoretical exploration of the debt person, Marx had a much more acute familiarity with it himself. If his notebook writings of the 1840s exposed the general subjectivation of the debtor, his personal life and letters expose its particular manifestation. In an exposition of Marx's economic problems, Peter Stallybrass (1998) starts out from the famous first chapters of *Das Kapital*, where linen and coats play important roles as objects of exchange. Marx's own coat was itself a constant object of exchange, pawned repeatedly to pay the family expenses. When it in the 1850s and 1860s was at the pawnbroker, Marx couldn't go to the British Library to work and earn money – or work on the chapters detailing the movements of the linen and coats in *Das Kapital* – because he didn't look presentable. The Marx household pawned all kinds of things and borrowed money from family and friends. Marx learned the humiliations of the "poor" which he years before had exposed theoretically. In a very material sense he shared the life experience of the working class, he fought for, living under precarious and changeable conditions, always without steady income enough to secure the family against the demands and accidents of life. In 1850 the family pawned some of the silverware that Jenny Marx had brought into the marriage from her family, and when Marx tried to pawn some more of it the plight of the uncreditworthy hit him. As the family friend Henry Hyndman described it:

> On one occasion Marx himself being in great need went out to pawn some household silver. He was not particularly well dressed and his knowledge of English was not as good as it became later. The silver, unfortunately, as it turned out, bore the crest of the Duke of Argyll's family, the Campbells, with which the house Mrs. Marx was directly connected. Marx arrived at the Bank of the Three Balls [pawnshop, three balls being its symbol] and produced his spoons and forks. Saturday night, foreign Jew, dress untidy, hair and beard roughly combed, handsome silver, noble crest – evidently a very suspicious transaction

> indeed. So thought the pawnbroker to whom Marx applied. He therefore detained Marx, one some pretext, while he sent for the police. The policeman took the same view as the pawnbroker and also took poor Marx to the police station. There again appearances were strongly against him [...] So Marx received the unpleasant hospitality of a police cell, while his anxious family mourned his disappearance (Quoted from McLellan 1981, 149).

The Marx family balanced on the edge of financial ruin and there is a remarkable letter from Marx to Friedrich Engels dated July 15, 1858. The letter itself is almost like one the documents on capitalism and the working class that Marx uses in *Das Kapital* and there is in this account of one family, as in the notebooks 15 years prior, a kind of sociological or moral philosophical exposure of the debt relation. Marx lives out the "poor" man's condition and the debtor's appearances and incantations. The letter starts with admonishing Engels not to be scared of its content because it "is not in any way intended as an appeal to your already unduly overloaded exchequer" (Marx 1983, 328 ["appeal" is written in English in the original German letter]). There is a prehistory, reminiscent of the debtor coming to borrow again, a debt relation already installed, an inequality that Marx refers to by dismissing it as relevant for this letter. Instead Marx articulate a somewhat more equal relation "to put our heads together to see if some way cannot be found out of the present situation, for it has become absolutely untenable" (ibid.).

The untenable situation consists in Marx having "to waste most of my time running round in fruitless attempts to raise money," making it impossible for him to work while making "a nervous wreck of my wife" (ibid.). The latter of which the doctor recommends cured by a spa resort that the family cannot afford. Marx is convinced the spa will have no positive effect "so long as she continues to be the victim of daily pressures and haunted by the spectre of final and unavoidable catastrophe" (ibid). After the first paragraph of the letter where Marx defines himself and his family as borrowers in desperate need, the next paragraph details his fruitless efforts to secure money from a loan society who lends money "*without securities* and on the strength of references alone" (ibid. ["securities" and "references" is written in English]). The attempt ended costing him 2 pounds on fees but no loan, illustrating the well-known saying that it is expensive to be poor. The paragraph ends by Marx contemplating trying again, and so now we have him as not only desperate but active, that is, in need and working, albeit unsuccessfully, to solve the situation.

He then turns to the letter's real centerpiece, an accounting made by Jenny Marx of the expenses paid with 20 pounds given earlier by Engels and 24 pounds made on journalistic work. This documentation is laid out in two accounts called "statement," one for each sum of money meticulously detailing expenses for water, gas, pawnshop interest, newspaper, clothes, baker etc., all the expenses of ordinary life. As shown by James Aho (2005) there is a profound connection between bookkeeping and confession, and in the letter Marx goes to great length to document the tally and to reassure Engels that from the statements "you will see that, as soon as a fairly substantial sum such as this arrives, not a penny is left over even for the most urgent day-to-day expenses, let alone enjoyment of any kind." Rather, "exactly the same sickening struggle recommences the following day" (Marx 1983, 329 ["struggle" is written in English]). He exposes, calculates and confesses the sorry state of the economic affairs and assures Engels of his complete lack of indulgence. Life is a struggle, as he says, and so he struggles. There is no rest or enjoyment. There is only the debtor life of securing funds, working hard and paying back loans. The debtor subjectivation is a moral bookkeeping tallied up in the two statements and the words surrounding it, a morality requiring a strict observance of income and expenses, an ability to discipline and supervise – and document – one's every move in accordance with the payback morality. The debtor is under constant suspicion of being lazy, indulgent and slothful and must therefore make his or her life transparent, orderly, and accountable for all (lender) eyes to see.

The two statements are followed by a third listing "the full state of indebtedness, as it now stands in London," followed by an explanation of the urgency related to each debtor post, remarking that the landlord "is himself being harried by creditors" (Marx 1983, 330). All the debtor post shows a system of credit and debt, where the payment of debt is not to secure a debt-free existence but to pay just so much that the credit line remains open: "Thus the whole business turns on the fact that what little comes in is never earmarked for the coming month, nor is it ever more than just sufficient [...] to reduce debts to a level that will preclude one's actually being thrown out into the street" (ibid). This is the eighteenth-century version of paying one credit card debt with another. In an almost one-to-one illustration of his Parisian thoughts in 1842 he now writes: "The show of respectability which has so far been kept up has been the only means of avoiding a collapse" (Marx 1983, 331 ["show of respectability" is written in English]), that is, wearing his coat outside, the children and wife looking decent, paying small amounts regularly, believable insurances of further repayments, appearances of credibility – counterfeiting the soul – all in the service of further indebtedness.

The final paragraph starts with a sentence in English: "I have now made a clean breast of it." He has exposed himself, detailed the inner life of his family, "and I assure you that it has cost me no small effort to do so" (ibid.). He has complied with the brutal logic of the debt relation and turned himself into an open (account) book.

10.3 The Measure of Self

The economic rationality of credit and debt is most visible because it tabulates the obligations in quantifiable numbers. "A debt is the obligation to pay a certain sum of money," David Graeber writes. "As a result, a debt, unlike any other form of obligation, can be precisely quantified" (2011, 13). The monetary debt is plain to see, the payment plan is there, the contractual parties are identified, the consequences of nonpayment is already stated, all of which makes for a very clear and comprehensible obligation. This tends, as evident even in the life world of capitalism's most formidable opponent, to translate into a moral obligation, into a payback morality, into core material for self-imagery.

Numbers are strong. They have a "capacity to turn morality into a matter of impersonal arithmetic" (ibid., 14). In his letter to Engels, Marx tries to use numbers to demonstrate the credibility of his character, but it is evident that these numbers are also used by his creditors to secure their payment and possibly to deny the Marx family further credit. The economic rationality of credit and debt are in the numbers. But they only become social reality and individual repayment by connecting with a moral rationality of credit and debt which recognizes honoring one's obligations, repayment, as the supreme measure of one's moral stature. To not repay one's moral obligations is to be a bad person. To not repay one's economic debt is to be a bad borrower but is also becomes to be a bad person, to be also inscribed within a moral register. This is why Marx makes so much of an effort when writing to his best friend, who knows all his troubles, of dispelling any notion of being a bad borrower. The credit line is the continuous calculation of moral character. It is the measure of the promissory person and, as Marx came to know, it tends also to become the measure of one self.

Bibliography

Aho, James. 2005. *Confession and Bookkeeping. The Religious, Moral, and Rhetorical Roots of Modern Accounting*. New York: State University of New York Press.

Calder, Lendol. 1999. *Financing the American Dream. A Cultural History of Consumer Credit*. Princeton/Oxford: Princeton University Press.

Graeber, David. 2011. *Debt. The first 5,000 years*. Brooklyn: Melville House.

Kamenetz, Anya. 2007. *Generation Debt*. New York: Riverhead Books.

Langley, Paul. 2008. *The Everyday Life of Global Finance*. Oxford: Oxford University Press.

Lazzarato, Maurizio. 2012. *The Making of the Indebted Man*. Los Angeles: Semiotext(e).

Martin, Randy. 2002. *Financialization of Daily Life*. Philadelphia: Temple University Press.

Marx, Karl. 1844. Comments on James Mill. *Éléments D'économie Politique*. www.marxists.org/archive/marx/works/1844/james-mill/index.htm. Accessed 19 July 2016.

———. 1983. Letter to Friedrich Engels, July 15, 1858. In *Karl Marx & Friedrich Engels Collected Works*, Vol. 40. London: Lawrence & Wishart.

McLellan, David. 1981. *Karl Marx: Interviews and Recollections*. London: Macmillan.

Stallybrass, Peter. 1998. Marx's Coat. In *Border Fetishisms. Material Objects in Unstable Spaces*, ed. P. Spyer, 183–207. New York/London: Routledge.

Chapter 11
Democratic Governance: A Genealogy

Mark Bevir

When governance refers to public organization and action, it surely captures one of the major trends of recent times. Many social scientists, especially those who work on public administration and local government, argue that the leading forms of public organization and action have shifted from hierarchic bureaucracies to markets and networks. Debates rage about the extent of this shift: bureaucratic hierarchies clearly remain widespread and arguably the most common forms of government. Questions may remain about the nature of the shift: have governments become less capable of getting their way or merely altered the ways in which they act? Yet, despite these doubts and questions, there is a widespread consensus that "governance" captures a shift in theory and practice towards markets and networks.

It is clear at least that successive governments have introduced wave after wave of public sector reform in their attempt to promote markets, contracting-out, networks, and joined-up government in place of hierarchic bureaucracy. This paper focuses on the intellectual sources of the transformation of the state and its relation to civil society. It highlights the role played in this transformation by modernist social science, with its reliance on formal explanations based on economic models or sociological correlations. Modernist social science informed the main narratives of the crisis of the administrative and welfare state in the 1970s. Modernist social science also inspired the two waves of public sector reform that responded to this crisis. In Britain, the first wave of reform was most prominent under Thatcherism, at which time an economic modernism inspired marketization and the new public management. The second wave of reform was most prominent under New Labour, at which time a sociological modernism inspired joined-up governance and networks.

In the late nineteenth century, social science was dominated by a developmental historicism that inspired grand narratives centered on the nation, the state, and

M. Bevir (✉)
Department of Political Science, University of California, Berkeley, CA 94720-1950, USA
e-mail: mbevir@berkeley.edu

J. Bek-Thomsen et al. (eds.), *History of Economic Rationalities*, Ethical Economy 54, DOI 10.1007/978-3-319-52815-1_11

Table 11.1 The rise and varieties of modernism

	Developmental historicism	Modernism	
		Government	The new governance
Concept of rationality	Civilizational	Economic and sociological	New theories of governance – rational choice and new institutionalism
State formation	Nation and/or Imperial state	Corporate and/or welfare state	Neoliberal and/or network state
Public sector	Civil service	Bureaucracy	New worlds of governance – markets and networks
Mode of accountability	Responsible government	Procedural accountability	Performance accountability

freedom. Developmental historicism appealed to narratives that situated events and institutions in a larger order of evolving continuity. Examples include Whig history, idealist philosophy, and evolutionary theorizing. The most significant feature of twentieth century social science was, in sharp contrast, the emergence of modernist modes of knowledge that atomize the flux of reality. Table 11.1 provides an overview.

The modernist break with developmental historicism had formal and substantive aspects (compare Everdell 1997; Porter 1995; Ross 1991, Chap. 8–10; Schabas 1990). In formal terms, modernists turned from historical narratives to formal models, correlations, and classifications that held across time and place. They explained outcomes by reference to psychological types, functional requirements of systems, a general human rationality, and ahistorical mechanisms and processes. In substantive terms, modernism overlapped with new emerging topics, including political parties, interest groups, and policy networks. The substantive and formal aspects of modernism often reinforced one another: the new techniques made it easier to study some of the new topics, and the new topics appeared to require new techniques for gathering and arranging data.

Modernist social science is dominated by two strands. Although the two strands of modernism contrast with developmental historicism, they instantiate different formal and ahistorical concepts of rationality associated with different forms of explanation and so different analyses of governance. On the one hand, the economic concept of rationality privileges utility maximization; it arose with neoclassical theory and spread to rational choice. On the other, the sociological concept of rationality privileges appropriateness in relation to social norms; it arose with functionalism and spread to network theory and communitarianism.

The economic concept of rationality found in neoclassical theory has a distinctive history. For much of the nineteenth century, economists merged analyses pioneered by Adam Smith with organic and historical themes. Neoclassical economics established its dominance only as developmental historicism gave way to modernism. Even then it did not obliterate other traditions. Historical and institutional economics continued to thrive, especially on the European continent where economists remained divided about the relevance of utility theory as late as the 1930s.[1] Nonetheless, the spread of modernism saw diachronic narratives of the development of economies, states, and civilizations give way to synchronic models and somewhat later rational choice theory (On the history of neoclassical economics and rational choice theory see Schabas 1990; Amadae 2003).

Neoclassical economics instantiates a concept of rationality suited to modernist emphases on atomization, deduction, and synchronic analyses. Economic rationality is a property of individual decisions and actions; it is not tied to norms, practices, or societies save in so far as these are judged effective or ineffective ways of aggregating individual choices. In addition, economic rationality is postulated as an axiom on the basis of which to construct deductive models; it is not deployed as a principle by which to interpret facts discovered through inductive empirical research. Finally, the models derived from the axioms of economic rationality are applied to general patterns irrespective of time and space; they do not trace the particular evolution of individuals, practices, or societies. A modernist view of knowledge set the scene for the economic concept of rationality, but the concept acquired its content from utility-maximization. In neoclassical economics, individuals act in order to maximize their personal utility, where utility is defined as a measure of the satisfaction gained from a commodity or other outcome.

The most prominent alternatives to the economic concept of rationality are a cluster of sociological ones, all of which replace instrumentality with appropriateness. Sociological rationality is about acting in accord with appropriate social norms to fulfill established roles in systems, processes, institutions, or practices. Some sociologists, including Emile Durkheim and Pierre Bourdieu, argue that even modern individuals are best conceived not as instrumental actors but as followers of social norms and roles. Others, including Max Weber and Herbert Marcuse, express fears about the spread of selfish, acquisitive, and instrumental norms in modern societies. These two strands of modernist sociology can come together in broad condemnations of modernity, capitalism, or consumerism for spreading selfish and instrumental norms that wreck older forms of solidarity and community.

It is worth noting that these sociological traditions with their alternative concepts of rationality date, like neoclassical economics, from the broad intellectual shift away from developmental historicism toward modernism with its emphasis on synchronic analyses. The commonalities of the economic and sociological concepts of rationality are just as important as their differences. Modernist economists and modernist sociologists compartmentalize aspects of social life so as to manage and explain facts. They seek to make sense of the particular not by locating it in a temporal narrative but by reducing it to formal mid-level or universal generalizations that allegedly hold across time and space. Sociologists might eschew deductive models, but they too reject narratives, preferring formal classifications, correlations, functions, systems, and ideal types. Although we can find functionalist themes in

[1] For a survey of the varied voices see the oft maligned but still useful T. Hutchison 1953. For an example of their debating public policy see *Royal Commission on the Depression of Trade and Industry, Final Report*, c. 4893/1886.

nineteenth century thinkers, formal sociological forms of explanation flourished only with the rise of modernism; it was Durkheim and Bronislaw Malinowski, not Auguste Comte and Herbert Spencer, who distinguished functional explanations that refer to the synchronic role of an object in a system or social order (a type of explanation they considered to be scientific) from both the psychological question of motivation and the historical question of origins.

The shift from developmental historicism to modernism altered the concept and nature of the state.[2] As modernists rejected historical narratives, so they challenged the concept of the state as arising out of a nation bound together by a common language, culture, and past. Modernists turned instead to formal patterns, regularities, or models of action and institutions across space and time. Again, when modernists turned away from a substantive focus on the state toward topics such as political parties, interest groups, and policy networks, these sub-state institutions were then studied in terms of laws or regularities derived, for example, from their functions in abstract systems. Even when modernists continued to study the state, they increasingly portrayed it as fragmented into factional interests associated with different classes or parties.

Modernism challenged the idea that representative democracy was a way of electing and holding to account politicians who would act in accord with the common good of a pre-political nation. Representative democracy was thus in danger of losing much of its legitimacy. However, modernist modes of knowledge opened up new ways of making and legitimating public policy in representative democracies. Modernist social science inspired a new belief in formal expertise. Public policy could be legitimate if it were based on the formal knowledge of modernist social science. Elected representatives no longer need express a national character and common good. They could define policy goals and check the activity of experts. Social scientists, professionals, and generalist civil servants would use their expertise to devise rational scientific policies in accord with these goals. Modernist social science thus helped to create the conditions for the administrative state.

One important justification for the creation and expansion of increasingly insulated and centralized bureaucracies was that they cured the abuses and irrationalities in democratic processes. Modernist social scientists, such as Mosei Ostrogrorski, Graham Wallas, and W. F. Willoughby, wrote of the factionalism, propaganda, and financial extravagances to which democratic governments were prone. Many believed an insulated and centralized bureaucracy could preserve democracy while removing its worst features – instability, irrationality, and sectarianism – from the day-to-day activities of governing. Corporatism and the welfare state were meant to overcome factionalism and irrationality. Under corporatism, the bureaucracy reached out to organized interests (Schmitter and Lehmbruch 1982). The corporatist state gave particular associations a privileged status as the representatives of social and economic groups. The privileged associations were involved in the formulation of public policy, and in return those associations helped to ensure the effective

[2] The rise of pluralist views of the state was especially pronounced in the US, on which see Gunnell 2004. For the British case see Runciman 2005 and Stears 2006.

implementation of the policies. The bureaucracy also reached out to individual citizens, assuming greater responsibility for their welfare.[3] The welfare state took control of the individual's health, education, pension, and unemployment insurance.

Governance arose out of a crisis in the modernist state. Over-simplifications will abound in any attempt to differentiate the plethora of ideas that fed into narratives about the crisis of the state in the late twentieth century. Nonetheless, one way of approaching these narratives is as the products of different modernist theories. Some narratives of the crisis of the state challenged bureaucracy, corporatism, and social welfare by drawing on the economic concept of rationality. Neoclassical micro-level assumptions informed, for example, narratives that tried to show fiscal crises were a pathology built into the welfare state. These narratives went as follows (King 1975). Citizens, being rational actors, try to maximize their short-term interests, privileging welfare policies that are of benefit to them as individuals over the long-term, cumulative, and shared effects of rising state expenditure. Similarly, politicians, being rational actors, try to maximize their short-term electoral interests, promoting policies that will gain the votes of these rational citizens rather than pursuing fiscal responsibility. Narrow political considerations thereby trump economic imperatives. Groups of voters demand more and more welfare benefits, and politicians constantly pass welfare legislation on behalf of these voters. A growing proportion of the national product goes on welfare, making fiscal crises inevitable. These narratives of state overload and state crisis pointed to a clear solution – fiscal austerity, monetary control, and a rolling-back of the state.

Other narratives of the crisis of the state drew on more sociological analyses of changes in the world.[4] These narratives implied that the state had to change in response to international and domestic pressures. Internationally, the increased mobility of capital made it more difficult for states to direct economic activity. The state could not go it alone, but rather had to pursue coordination and regulation across borders. Industries that had operated in the domain of the state became increasingly transnational in their activities. The increasing number and prominence of transnational corporations raised problems of coordination and questions of jurisdiction. There was a gap between the national operation of regulatory structures and an increasingly international economy. Domestically, the state confronted the rising demands of its citizens. These demands arose from popular discontent with the state's handling of the economy and its apparent unresponsiveness. Many states were saddled with large debts. Globalization provoked anxieties about competitiveness and wages. Sections of the public worried that the state had lost control. Equally, state-actors often found they were subject to varied and even contradictory demands from the public. Voters wanted better services and lower taxes. They wanted a more effective state but also a more transparent and accountable one. They wanted decisive leaders and yet more popular participation.

---

[3] For discussions of the growing role of expertise from the nineteenth century to the early spread of social welfare see MacLeod 1988.

[4] For discussion see Bevir 2005 and Finlayson 1999.

The new governance consists of the interconnected theories and reforms by which people conceived of the crisis of the state and responded to it. These theories and reforms rejected the expertise associated with the post-War state. However, instead of challenging the idea of applying modernist expertise to social life, policy actors turned to alternative modernist modes of knowing to sustain new forms of expertise. Governance then rose in two analytically distinct waves of public sector reform. The first wave of reforms echoed an economic concept of rationality; neoliberalism promoted the new public management and contracting-out. The second wave echoed a sociological concept of rationality; the Third Way promoted joined-up governance, networks, and partnerships.

A first wave of reforms drew on public dissatisfaction with bureaucracy, and also on neoliberalism and rational choice theory, both of which explained and legitimated this dissatisfaction. Neoliberals compared the state's top-down, hierarchical mode of organization with the decentralized, competitive structure of the market. They argued that the market was superior. They concluded that when possible markets or quasi-markets should replace bureaucracy. A quest for efficiency led them to call on the state to transfer organizations and activities to the private sector. Organizations could be transferred by privatization, that is, the transfer of state assets to the private sector through flotations or management buy-outs. Activities could be transferred by means of contracting-out, that is, the state could pay a private sector organization to undertake tasks on its behalf.

Most neoliberals combined their faith in markets with a faith that the discipline of the market must somehow validate the management practices of the private sector. They redefined public officials as managers or service-providers, and they redefined citizens as consumers or service-users. More specifically, neoliberal reforms of the public sector often reflected formal analyses. Neoclassical economists first developed principal-agent theory to analyze the problem of delegated discretion in the private sector (Stiglitz 1987). They argued that delegating decision-making from principals (shareholders) to agents (managers) is risky because the agents may act on their own interests. Economists proposed minimizing this risk by using incentives and market mechanisms to align the interests of the agents with those of the principals. In the public sector, the principals are the voters and their elected representatives while the agents are public officials. For rational choice theorists, therefore, as the basic problem of private sector corporations was to ensure managers acted on behalf of the shareholders, so the basic problem of public administration was to ensure public officials work on behalf of citizens. Neoliberals extended to the public sector the incentives and market mechanisms that economists had devised to bring the interests of agents into alignment with those of their principals. The result was the new public management (Barzelay 2001; Pollitt and Bouckaert 2000).

Popular and neoliberal narratives combined with more formal analyses to produce a paradigm shift within modernism. The new paradigm denounced bureaucracy and public officials, and championed markets and entrepreneurs. It turned away from what was now derided as big government, bloated bureaucracy, and uniform solutions, and toward a private sector that was now lauded as competitive, efficient, and flexible. This paradigm shift was also one from institutional definitions of good government, which emphasized clear-cut divisions of responsibility within hierarchical relationships, toward new definitions of efficient processes defined in terms of service-delivery and outputs with an attendant emphasis on transparency, user-friendliness, and incentive structures.

When social scientists inspired by sociological theories of rationality studied neoliberal reforms of the public sector, they were often highly critical. They argued that the reforms exasperated problems of coordination and steering; they promoted networks and joined-up government (Rhodes 1997). Advocates of networks distinguish them from hierarchies as well as markets. Old institutionalists believed that hierarchies made it easier to tackle many social problems by dividing them into smaller tasks each of which could then be performed by a specialized unit. New institutionalists argue that this hierarchic approach to problem-solving no longer suits today's world. They claim that policy makers confront "wicked problems" that are not amenable to division and specialization; to solve today's problems requires networks.

The concept of a "wicked problem" rose as part of an amorphous mid-range social science associated with institutionalism, organization theory, and functionalism (Rittel and Webber 1973). Social democratic governments then picked up and adopted it to counter the ideas and policies of neoliberals. Wicked problems are usually defined in terms such as: a problem of more or less unique nature; the lack of any definitive formulation of such a problem; the existence of multiple explanations for it; the absence of a test to decide the value of any response to it; all responses to it being better or worse rather than true or false; and each response to it has important consequences such that there is no real chance to learn by trial and error. Typically these features strongly imply that wicked problems are interrelated. For example, a particular wicked problem might be explained in terms of its relationship to others, or any response to it might impact others. Classic examples of wicked problems include pressing issues of governance such as security, environment, and urban blight.

Institutionalists usually accept neoliberal arguments about the inflexible and unresponsive nature of hierarchies, but instead of promoting markets, they appeal to networks as a suitably flexible and responsive alternative based on recognition that social actors operate in structured relationships. They argue that efficiency and effectiveness derive from stable relationships characterized by trust, social participation, and voluntary associations. In their view, while hierarchies can provide a context for trust and stability, the time for hierarchies has passed. Hierarchies do not suit the new knowledge-driven global economy. This new world increasingly throws up wicked problems that require networks and joined-up governance. A new institutionalism, with its sociological concept of rationality, thus inspired a second wave of reforms, including not only many of New Labour's policies but also Australia's whole-of-government agenda, international attempts to deal with failed states, and post-9/11 security policy in the US (Bevir 2010).

The problem with most discussions of public servants under the new governance is that they rely on similar modernist assumptions to those that have inspired the turn to markets and networks. These modernist accounts of the new governance typically imply that we can define the new governance by reference to one or more essential property. They imply that these properties are general ones that characterise all cases of the new governance: we find governance in its contemporary guise if and only if we find a spread of networks. They also imply that these essential properties can explain at least the most significant other features of the new governance.

Surely, however, it is only modernist social science that makes these implications seem at all plausible. Really practices of governance are the products of people's activity, and people's activity is not determined by institutional norms or a logic of modernisation but by their situated agency. Really governance is constructed differently by numerous actors grappling with different issues in different contexts against the background of different traditions. In practice, therefore, the attempts by policy-makers to introduce markets and networks have met with complex patterns of resistance from public servants, street level bureaucrats, and citizens all inspired by local traditions that challenge and transform understandings rooted in modernist social science. From this perspective, governance is far from monolithic. Instead of looking for comprehensive accounts and explanations of the new governance, we might accept that it varies widely from case to case. The new governance is a complex policy environment in which an increasing range of actors forge various practices in reaction to the spread of policies, inspired by modernist social science, which seek to establish markets and networks.

The administrative and welfare state of the mid-twentieth century is starting to look as if it might have had a relatively short shelf-life. The initial turn to an ethic of welfare occurred within nineteenth century thought. Idealist philosophy, immanentist theology, and humanitarian positivism all helped sustain a concern with brotherhood, fellowship, and social duty. Arguably, however, this ethic had only limited impact on public policy. The administrative and welfare state depended not only on the persistence of this ethic but at least as much on the rise of new modernist expertise. It was modernist expertise that guided state bureaucracy as it expanded its range into ever wider areas of social life.

By the late twentieth century, however, modernist expertise itself had undermined faith in bureaucracy. Some policy makers may have rejected an ethic of welfare, others may have clung to one, but almost all of them rejected hierarchic organization. Whether they wanted to promote entrepreneurial individualism or civic spirit, they sought to do so through new forms of public organization and public action. They turned to markets and networks. Still, their policies have not worked as the policy makers intended. Instead, the world of hierarchies and bureaucratic norms has persisted even as it has been overlain by some features of markets and networks. Senior civil servants, agency managers, street-level bureaucrats, and citizens all confront a confusing and unmanageable set of demands reflecting an ever proliferating number of reforms and directives. Each of them muddles through. And it is their muddling through that then creates the practices of governance in which we now find ourselves.

Bibliography

Amadae, S.M. 2003. *Rationalizing Capitalist Democracy: The Cold War Origins of Rational Choice Liberalism*. Chicago: University of Chicago Press.
Barzelay, Michael. 2001. *The New Public Management*. Berkeley: University of California Press.
Bevir, Mark. 2005. *New Labour: A Critique*. London: Routledge.
———. 2010. *Democratic Governance*. Princeton: Princeton University Press.
Everdell, William. 1997. *The First Moderns*. Chicago: University of Chicago Press.
Finlayson, Alan. 1999. Third Way Theory. *Political Quarterly* 70: 271–279.
Gunnell, John. 2004. *Imagining the American Polity: Political Science and the Discourse of Democracy*. University Park: Pennsylvania State University Press.
Hutchison, Terence W. 1953. *A Review of Economic Doctrines, 1870–1929*. Oxford: Clarendon Press.
King, Anthony. 1975. Overload: Problems of Governing in the 1970s. *Political Studies* 23: 284–296.
MacLeod, Roy, ed. 1988. *Government and Expertise: Specialists, Administrators, and Professionals, 1860–1919*. Cambridge: Cambridge University Press.
Pollitt, Cristopher, and Geert Bouckaert. 2000. *Public Management Reform: A Comparative Analysis*. Oxford: Oxford University Press.
Porter, Theodore M. 1995. *Trust in Numbers: The Pursuit of Objectivity in Science and Public Life*. Princeton: Princeton University Press.
Rhodes, R.A.W. 1997. *Understanding Governance*. Buckingham: Open University Press.
Rittel, Horst, and Melvin Webber. 1973. Dilemmas in a General Theory of Planning. *Policy Sciences* 4: 155–169.
Ross, Dorothy. 1991. *The Origins of American Social Science*. Cambridge: Cambridge University Press.
Royal Commission on the Depression of Trade and Industry, Final Report, c. 4893/1886.
Runciman, David. 2005. *Pluralism and the Personality of the State*. Cambridge: Cambridge University Press.
Schabas, Margaret. 1990. *A World Ruled by Number: William Stanley Jevons and the Rise of Mathematical Economics*. Princeton: Princeton University Press.
Schmitter, Phillippe, and Gerhard Lehmbruch. 1982. *Patterns of Corporatist Policy Making*. London: Sage.
Stears, Marc. 2006. *Progressives, Pluralists, and the Problems of the State: Ideologies of Reform in the United States and Britain, 1909–1926*. Oxford: Oxford University Press.
Stiglitz, Joseph. 1987. Principal and Agent. *The New Palgrave: A Dictionary of Economics* 3: 966–971.

Chapter 12
The Economic De-Legitimization and Legitimization of Arts Policies 1970–1985

Erwin Dekker

12.1 Introduction

In 1953 Lionel Robbins addressed an audience of art lovers at a meeting in Birmingham. He spoke enthusiastically about the role of the arts in a liberal society. Robbins argued that in a world of diminished differences in wealth the government should take up the role of patron and support the arts, just like the governments of the Renaissance Italian city-states and that of ancient Athens had done. The state can encourage the arts and create a milieu in which the arts can flourish in harmony with "the principles of a free society:" "The market mechanism is a splendid thing for ministering to wants and satisfactions which can be discretely formulated. But we oversimplify and run the risk of discrediting a fundamental institution, if we claim that it can formulate demands for all the necessary ingredients of the good society" (Robbins 1958/1963, 58–9). Robbins was not alone in that view. The Arts Council in Britain had been set up with the help of John Maynard Keynes who argued that:

> The purpose of the Arts Council of Great Britain is to create an environment, to breed a spirit, to cultivate an opinion, to offer a stimulus to such purpose that the artist and the public can each sustain and live on the other in that union which has occasionally existed in the past at the great ages of communal civilised life (quoted in Blake 1997, 59).

In the United States John Kenneth Galbraith in his *Economics and the Quality of Life* argued that social goods, such as the arts, were of increasing importance in a world in which private consumption was losing economic priority (Galbraith 1963/2001). They argued that it was one of the functions of the welfare state to promote the arts.

During the 1970s a community of economists of the arts, located in the United States and United Kingdom, emerges which turns the debate over public support to the

---

E. Dekker (✉)
Erasmus School of History, Culture & Communication, Rotterdam, The Netherlands
e-mail: e.dekker@eshcc.eur.nl

J. Bek-Thomsen et al. (eds.), *History of Economic Rationalities*, Ethical Economy 54, DOI 10.1007/978-3-319-52815-1_12

arts into a question of justifications for specific subsidies. They were unsatisfied with a generic case for support to the arts, and more interested in rigorous justifications for specific policies (Hendon et al. 1980a). During this decade these economists of the arts met regularly and their discussion quickly centered on the justification for arts subsidies.[1] The tone of their contributions was often tough, as one of the prominent contributors David Cwi confidently argued: "People will want some hard answers as to how they benefit when their tax dollars are used to support activities they do not believe are meritorious" (Cwi 1980, 66). Subsidies had to be cost-effective, a sentiment that was echoed in the 1977 report of the British Arts Council "Value for Money."

This shift from a generic case for support to the arts as an essential part of a modern welfare state, to the justification of specific subsidies did not go unnoticed. Advocates of the cultural sector and social philosophers objected vehemently to this strong but narrow logic. They tried to oppose the imperialism of the economists into the arts (Blaug 1976). These economists of the arts, among them Mark Blaug, Alan Peacock, Bill Hendon and William Baumol, to the contrary felt that they were providing a sounder basis for the justification of subsidies to the arts (Hendon et al. 1980a, xii).

This paper will analyze that shift in the discourse and the justification of support for the arts between 1970 and 1985 in the Anglo-Saxon world. It will do this by analyzing three skirmishes between economists and those working in the arts field or in neighboring social sciences. This paper will show that these debates revolved around the position of art in society and the relation of democratic decision making, to market institutions and consumer sovereignty. The first debate we will discuss is between economist of the arts Mark Blaug and prominent member of the Arts Council Richard Findlater, following a controversial piece published in the British left-leaning literary magazine *Encounter*. The debate is about the (perceived) need for the Arts Council in Britain to specify its aims so that economists can evaluate their efforts. The second debate takes place between political scientist F.F. Ridley who takes the cultural economists to task for failing to understand the nature of politics. The third debate involves the notion of merit goods and is ultimately about the importance of the arts. By examining these debates this chapter sheds light on how purely economic arguments came to dominate justifications for support to the arts, and how this economic rationality was challenged when it was first put forward. By economic rationality I mean here the justification of state policies that relies on purely economic arguments.

12.2 Evaluating the Arts Council

In what Mark Blaug and his co-author Karen King called an "iconoclastic essay" they take the Arts Council in Britain, the main distributive agency for government funds directed to the arts, to task for not making clear what its aims and objectives

[1] Two publications stand out: the special issue of the Journal of Economic Behavior, summer 1977 and the edited volume by Hendon, Shanahan and MacDonald 'Economic Policy for the Arts' (1980).

are, thereby making it impossible to evaluate their policies (King and Blaug 1973/1976a, 1973/1976b). In line with what Blaug has elsewhere called the "technocratic perspective" they argue that the primary task of the economist is to evaluate the efficiency with which means have been employed to achieve the policy objectives set out by politicians or policy makers (Blaug 1992, 128–9). In the absence of such objectives there is no way to find out what whether the money has been spent in a "cost-effective" manner. It is important to observe that this technocratic perspective is neutral with regards to the goal of these policies, or as King and Blaug put it: "in the final analysis artistic judgments are subjective, and so are the objectives that underlie all expenditures on the Arts. What is *not* subjective, however is the degree to which spending on one activity rather than another achieves a particular objective" (King and Blaug 1973/1976a, 120).

King and Blaug have sifted through the policy proposals and other documents published by the Arts Council in search of consistent objectives, but in vain they argue. If they could find a goal of policy it was vaguely formulated and frequently contradicted within the same document. Trade-offs between goals such as promoting new artists and attracting new audiences were not made explicit. From the essay it becomes clear that the language of the reports makes King and Blaug especially impatient, they look for "objective selection criteria" and "rational judgments" but instead they find a "lack of criteria" and "glaring inconsistencies." They are puzzled by generic statements that the "preservation of the fine arts is a collective responsibility" which, they argue, provides no guide for policy at all (King and Blaug 1973/1976a).

The response, also published in *Encounter*, by Richard Findlater, member of the Arts Council and one of England's premier theatre critics at the time, is a defense of the expert-based policy making procedures of the Arts Council. First Findlater argues that the decisions and judgments of the Arts Council have always been formed pragmatically rather than on strict principles. The refusal to apply strict principles or to put those in print, Findlater argues: "[should not] be regarded, a la King and Blaug, as a sign of moral cowardice and intellectual confusion […] English committees are bound to compromise, intellectually; they don't dictate and they can't prescribe […] For me, that's a saving grace, if the relative – if diminishing – freedoms of the arts are not to suffer further interference from the state" (Findlater 1973/1976, 129). He argues that the decisions of the Council are bound to differ when the leadership changes, or indeed when the government does. Findlater furthermore argues that the Arts Council has contributed to a positive change in attitude towards the arts and their patronage both in society as well as in government in line with the goal of creating a milieu in which the arts could flourish as suggested by Keynes and Robbins.

The debate is telling for the perceived differences in what policy making looks like. Findlater appreciates and praises the political art of muddling through while Blaug and King demand transparency and consistency. It is a clash between the expertise and standing of the members of the Arts Council – Findlater invokes various Sir's – who regard themselves as patrons of the arts and the demand for rational policy making based on firm justifications and clear trade-offs by Blaug and King. What distinguishes this debate from the other debates, however, is that King and

Blaug never actually challenge the legitimacy of support for the arts or that of the Arts Council as a political body; they merely criticize its behavior, especially its unwillingness to make the relevant trade-offs explicit.

12.3 Preferences and Political Values

The legitimacy of support for the arts is at stake for political scientist F.F. Ridley in his indictment of the economists of the arts in their own *Journal of Cultural Economics*. Ridley claims:

> Though its [economics of the arts'] central concern seems to be the issue of subsidies – the circumstances in which state patronage of the arts is justified – the case made is so limited that those who believe culture to be an essential element of a civilized nation may be well advised to avoid an alliance with econo*mics altogether* (Ridley 1983: 1).

Ridley is not alone in his concerns. In the preface to a collection of papers that was the outcome of the first conference that brought economists of the arts together with practitioners and policy makers in Edinburgh in 1978, it is argued that: "To practitioners and scholars in the humanities, economists must surely look like rigorous and precise thinkers who nonetheless believe firmly in their premises without fully examining them and without admitting other premises [...] economists argue from a narrow but strong logic" (Hendon et al. 1980a, xii). But the main bone of contention for Ridley is not this narrow logic, to which we will return in the next section, but rather the philosophical assumption that "individual choices are the touchstone of what is desirable and that the goals of public policy should therefore be to maximize their satisfaction" (Ridley 1983, 3). He argues for a distinction between individual choices and values, but instead he finds in the work of economists the arts the denial of any difference between the two. Values, for the economists, are mere expressions of personal preference. As another contributor to the Edinburgh conference, David Austen-Smith argues: "The problem of justifying subsidies in the arts is an important one in supposedly liberal-democratic societies where any redistribution of resources solely on grounds of taste is generally considered illegitimate" (Austen-Smith 1980, 24).

If political and cultural values are mere expressions of personal preference, any attempt to correct or alter those reeks of paternalism.[2] Baumol and Bowen, who wrote the book that arguably started the economics of the arts *Performing Arts: The Economic Dilemma* (1966), arrive at this conclusion via an interesting kind of populism:

> To the man in the street, however, this [an appeal to the inherent value of beauty and the ineffable contribution of aesthetic activity] may not be an acceptable answer. Indeed, it is likely to smack of things he rightly considers dangerous: paternalism, dictatorship of tastes and *violation of consumer sovereignty* (Baumol and Bowen 1966, 48).

[2]The emphasis on personal preferences can also be found in Blaug's introduction (1976) to the economics of the arts and in the work of prominent economist of the art Alan Peacock, see below.

That is not to say that Baumol and Bowen or Austen-Smith completely oppose state support of the arts, it is rather that they attempt to find different, more firm, ground for it.

Ridley, instead, argues that decision making in liberal democracies can be justified without relying directly on personal preferences. A political consensus, he argues, consists of more than a counting of hands or a popular vote, liberal democracies frequently recognize principles (Justice, Freedom) that do not depend on popular opinion (alone) for their validity, and he argues that the arts are of a similar kind. Politicians, moreover, are entrusted with certain responsibilities which allow them to implement policies which (at least in isolation) are not always supported by a popular majority. Or in the words of Edmund Burke, which Ridley quotes approvingly: "Your representative owes you his judgement; and he betrays you, instead of serving your if he sacrifices it to public opinion [...] Government and legislation are matters of reason, judgement, and not of inclination" (Burke quoted in Ridley 1983, 7).

Ridley develops this point into a more general criticism of economics. The failure to recognize values that extend beyond the individual and political goals such as "the promotion of the good, the true and the beautiful" leads them astray he argues. Ridley instead argues that any substantive notion of the "good" or the "right" can never rely purely on what people want, their preferences, it also consists of what individuals believe to be good or right, on a concept of justice.[3] This contrast comes out most clearly in the debate surrounding "the merit good," which emerges as the crucial difference between economists of the arts and its critics.

12.4 Consumer Sovereignty and Merit Goods

Much of the debate during the 1970s came to be centered on the "merit good" argument first put forward by, the founding father of modern public finance, Richard Musgrave in 1957. Merit goods are goods that are for some reason intrinsically valued. The merit good argument was and is still used as an argument to justify government support of the arts. Both sides of the debate, however, were unhappy with the argument. Ridley and others thought of it as bad economic interpretation of their argument that the arts were essential to society, while (most) of the economists of the arts felt it was, well, bad economics and a violation of consumer sovereignty.

For those sympathetic to the arts the value of art hardly needed further demonstration. One might inquire into what beauty is, just like scientists inquire what truth is, and political philosophers inquire into the nature of the good, but the importance of beauty itself was never questioned. The importance of such "goods" and their distinguished place in (liberal) society was taken for granted. It was a line of reasoning that we also encountered in Robbins, Keynes and Galbraith in the introduction.

[3] In recent years economists of the arts have become more appreciative of such values, they now recognize non-use values such as option, existence and bequest values (Frey 2003).

This argument was interpreted and reformulated as the "merit good" argument by the economists of the art. Some goods were special and they should not just be available for those willing or able to pay, but they should be available to all members of the community. Economists of the arts, however, immediately were very critical of this argument. In the conference proceedings of the first conference on the arts and economics the editors are clear:

> The merit good argument is a political argument, not an economic one, a point that has needed to be made for some time. For public monies to be used for arts subsidies, we must be able to show either that the public interest will be served directly or at least that the special interests served are widely accepted as desirable social objectives (Hendon et al. 1980b, 21).

In her recent *Handbook of Cultural Economics* (2003) Ruth Towse is a little more subtle, but the fundamental mistrust of the merit good argument remains (notice also the quotation marks around merit): "'merit' goods [is] the term used by economists for goods that are held, usually by experts, to have inherent value for society" (Towse 2003, 3).[4]

The economic criticism of the merit good argument is telling for at least two reasons. Firstly it emphasizes the neutrality of economists who in contrast to other "experts" can give neutral advice on the means to achieve policy objectives, and who remain far from "political arguments." Secondly as Ridley emphasized they adopt a populist stance in line with "the man in the street" which Baumol and Bowen invoked or in line with the public interest as opposed to special interests. By then they have not only downgraded support of the arts to a special interest, but also claimed that those "experts" seeking to promote the arts give political advice, rather than neutral "scientific" advice that economists can provide. This rhetorical strategy is also adopted by, art enthusiast and one of the most prominent public economists of the arts in Britain, Alan Peacock:

> Subsidizing the Arts involves the same kind of issues as subsidizing particular industries or services in the economy [...] Cultural paternalism which might be justified on the grounds that the community does not know what is good for it, is ruled out. Apart from any predisposition of the author to oppose paternalism, the assertion of imposed value judgements is too easy a way of deriving support for public intervention designed to give the public not what it wants but what it ought to have! (Peacock 1969/1994, 151).

The most striking part of this quotation is undoubtedly "too easy." It shows what the economists felt they were doing: trying to derive an objective (economic) justification for support to the arts. What they met however, was primarily misunderstanding and bafflement as exemplified by the responses of Ridley, Findlater and that of the British establishment to the report written about the cost-effectiveness of British orchestras (Towse 2005). Enthusiasts of the arts felt that the relative importance of the arts was the core of the issue. What the economists instead did was to sidestep that importance and to attempt to derive justifications for public support via the way of market failures and positive externalities. Peacock's starting point is the primacy of markets and the sacredness of consumer sovereignty. It is this assumption which is fundamentally challenged by the critics of the economists of the arts. And it is an assumption that has

[4] For an early exception Scitovsky (1972)

frequently created some unease among economists of the arts themselves. A variety of them have claimed that the formation of tastes should become an important object of study (see Blaug 2001). It has nonetheless been largely neglected as the overview of the subject by Blaug shows. This provokes Ridley to argue that: "the old tag 'de gustibus non est disputandum' is clearly illogical. The fact that so many economists have made it their credo is a coward's escape from the question that must lie at the start of any exercise" (Ridley 1983, 17). The critics find taste and the cultivation of the appreciation for art too important an issue to leave to others, while economists of the arts have found it too "political" or "difficult" an issue to study.

12.5 Conclusion

What we have analyzed above is the clash of a micro-economic rationality that was part of the economics imperialism movement of the postwar period with the established discourse of arts as an essential part of a civilized society. In the confrontation between Findlater on the one hand and Blaug on the other the issue of transparency of decision-making and the accountability of the government is at stake. King and Blaug claim that the Arts Council is unaccountable because it is unwilling to state its goals, Findlater attempts to defend the pragmatism and the expertise of the Arts Council. In that sense Ridley's contribution can be seen as a counter-attack, which attempts to establish the primacy of politics. He attempts to establish autonomy for legislators in their policies, but his case for support for the arts remains generic. Whereas the micro-economic reasoning excels is in the domain of specific policies and the extent that these policies should have, the established discourse relies more on a general defense of state patronage to the arts.

In the discussion of the merit good the contrast between the rationalities is stark. The older rationality is that of the good civilized society of which the arts are a natural part. That in itself is not an argument for support to the arts, but is interpreted as such during a period in which the welfare-state is taken for granted. The economists are unwilling to accept this argument, they feel it is completely backwards: it assumes the need for support rather than providing proof and evidence for it. The natural starting point for them is the self-governing market with sovereign consumers and a deviation from this starting point needs to be justified. The economists of the arts believe that this will make the case for support of the arts stronger, but the critics are afraid it will hollow out the rationale for such support in the first place. For if we do not support the arts to achieve excellence, but to correct some market failure are we still doing it for the right reason?

That question is of particular relevance in the following decades in which the primary reason for support to the creative and cultural industries becomes that they help the economy grow or help generate social cohesion (Belfiore 2004). That demonstrates that there is no easy choice between the older discourse and the new "economics of the arts" rationality, they are frequently are cross-purposes. The economic rationality succeeded in challenging the legitimacy and the extent to which the arts deserved support, but it did so by side-stepping some of the most difficult issues:

what is excellence in the arts (by measuring secondary social and economic effects) and what importance should be attached to consumer preferences (by assuming consumer sovereignty). This caused frustration among non-economists who believed that these were the issues that were most important in the first place.

Bibliography

Austen-Smith, David. 1980. On Justifying Subsidies to the Performing Arts. In *Economic Policy for the Arts*, ed. William S. Hendon, James L. Shanahan, and Alice J. MacDonald, 24–31. Cambridge, MA: Abt Books.

Baumol, William J., and W.G. Bowen. 1966. *Performing Arts: The Economic Dilemma*. New York: Twentieth Century Fund.

Belfiore, E. 2004. Auditing Culture. *International Journal of Cultural Policy* 10: 183–202.

Blake, Andrew. 1997. *The Land Without Music*. Manchester: Manchester University Press.

Blaug, Mark. 1976. Introduction: What is the Economics of the Arts About. In *The Economics of the Arts*, 13–22. London: Martin Robertson.

———. 1983. Justifications for Subsidies to the Arts: A Reply to F.F. Ridley. *Journal of Cultural Economics* 7: 19–22.

———. 1992. *The Methodology of Economics*. Cambridge: Cambridge University Press.

———. 2001. Where are we Now on Cultural Economics? *Journal of Economic Surveys* 15: 123–143.

Cwi, David. 1980. Public Support of the Arts: Three Arguments Examined. *Journal of Cultural Economics* 4: 39–68.

Findlater, Richard. 1973/1976. The Arts Council and its Critics. In *The Economics of the Arts*, ed. Mark Blaug, 126–129. London: Martin Robertson.

Frey, Bruno S. 2003. *Arts & Economics: Analysis and Cultural Policy*. Berlin: Springer.

Galbraith, John Kenneth. 1963/2001. Economics and the Quality of Life. In *The Essential Galbraith*, ed. Andrea D. Williams, 90–108. Boston: Houghton Mifflin.

Hendon, William S., James L. Shanahan, and Alice J. MacDonald. 1980a. Preface. In *Economic Policy for the Arts*, ed. William S. Hendon, James L. Shanahan, and Alice J. MacDonald, ix–xiii. Cambridge, MA: Abt Books.

———. 1980b. Introduction to Public Support for the Arts. In *Economic Policy for the Arts*, ed. William S. Hendon, James L. Shanahan, and Alice J. MacDonald, 21–23. Cambridge, MA: Abt Books.

King, Karen, and Mark Blaug. 1973/1976a. Does the Arts Council Know What it is Doing. In *The Economics of the Arts*, ed. Mark Blaug, 101–125. London: Martin Robertson.

———. 1973/1976b. A Reply. In *The Economics of the Arts*, ed. Mark Blaug, 127–129. London: Martin Robertson.

Peacock, Alan T. 1969/1994. Welfare Economics and Public Subsidies to the Arts. *Journal of Cultural Economics* 18: 151–161.

Ridley, F.F. 1983. Cultural Economists and the Culture of Economists. *Journal of Cultural Economics* 7: 1–18.

Robbins, Lionel R. 1958/1963. Art and the State. In *Politics and Economics: Papers in Political Economy*, ed. Lord Robbins, 53–72. London: Macmillan and Co..

Scitovsky, Tibor. 1972. What's Wrong with the Arts is What's Wrong with Society. *The American Economic Review* 62: 62–69.

Towse, Ruth. 2003. Introduction. In *Handbook of Cultural Economics*, ed. Ruth Towse, 1–14. Cheltenham: Edward Elgar.

Towse, R. 2005. Alan Peacock and Cultural Economics. *The Economic Journal* 115: F262–F276.

Chapter 13
From "Health for All" to "Health as Investment:" The Role of Economic Rationalities in the Transition from International to Global Health 1978–2013

Katherine E. Kenny

13.1 Introduction

The last 25 years have witnessed a dramatic shift in the terrain of world health. Usually characterized as a transition from "international" to "global" health, this shift has been accompanied by epidemiological, organizational, geopolitical and financial transformations. Even though global health has emerged as the dominant term for attempts to address matters of health and disease on a transnational scale, how it differs from earlier designations such as international health or tropical medicine remains underspecified (Anderson 2014; Banta 2001; Brown et al. 2006; Fried et al. 2010; Kleinman 2010; Koplan et al. 2009; Lakoff 2010; McGoey et al. 2011). Scholars have observed a number of features that have accompanied the rise of global health: the declining role of the World Health Organization (WHO) dating from the budget freezes of the 1980s, the relative ascendance of the World Bank in world health affairs, the proliferation of public private partnerships, Bill Gates-style philanthrocapitalism, and an emphasis on health threats that transcend national boundaries, i.e. HIV/AIDs, SARS, pandemic influenza and, more recently, the ebola virus (Brown et al. 2006; Chorev 2012; Kenny 2015; Lakoff and Collier 2008; McCarthy 2002; McCoy et al. 2009; Ruger 2005; Thomas and Weber 2004). In this paper I identify a less frequently observed feature: the rise of non-communicable diseases (NCDs) as a global health concern. NCDs, also known as "chronic" or "lifestyle" diseases,

---

This chapter contains excerpts that have previously appeared in print. See Katherine Kenny 'The Biopolitics of Global Health: Life and death in neoliberal time' Journal of Sociology 51(1) pp. 9–27. Copyright ©2015 by The Australian Sociological Association. Reprinted by permission of SAGE Publications, Ltd.

K.E. Kenny (✉)
Practical Justice Initiative, School of Social Sciences, University of New South Wales, Sydney, Australia
e-mail: katherine.kenny@unsw.edu.au

J. Bek-Thomsen et al. (eds.), *History of Economic Rationalities*, Ethical Economy 54, DOI 10.1007/978-3-319-52815-1_13

include conditions such as cardiovascular disease, cancer, respiratory disease and diabetes and share four common risk factors: tobacco use, physical inactivity, alcohol consumption and unhealthy diet. I argue that the current concern with NCDs, and the transition from international to global health more generally, coincides with the historical rise of economic rationalities in the field of world health over the last 25 years.

I begin by comparing two prominent moments in the history of world health – the 1978 Alma-Ata Declaration, in which the WHO reaffirmed its commitment to the goal of "health for all by the year 2000," and the 2013 High Level Meeting of the UN General Assembly at which Non-communicable Diseases were declared to be a grave threat to the global economy. The contrast between these two moments illustrates the central question of this chapter: How did the dominant conceptualization of health shift from a legitimate end in itself to something that should be maximized in service to the economy?

I answer this question by locating the origins of global health in the structural and conceptual transformations of the field of world health that began immediately following the Alma-Ata conference. I then focus on the World Bank's increasing involvement in world health affairs beginning in the late 1980s and culminating in the publication of the World Development Report 1993: Investing in Health. In addition to its widely criticized recommendations for health sector financing (emphasizing privatization of health care services), the Investing in Health report also introduced a new way of conceptualizing health using the disability adjusted life year (DALY) metric. One DALY is equivalent to a *year* of *healthy life* lost to either premature death or to disability. It represents an internationally standardized quantum of ill health used to measure the global incidence of health and disease and to perform cost-effective analyses on potential health care interventions. The shift from disease-specific mortality statistics to DALY calculations brought the global burden of NCDs into clear focus. However, the DALY method by which NCDs became a global health priority relies on a particular *economic* valuing of human life.[1] I situate the creation of the DALY metric with respect to the broader field of health economics, which itself emerged through the 1970s and 1980s. I argue that the DALY metric explains the rise of NCDs on the global health agenda and, more fundamentally, illustrates the rise economic rationalities in the field of global health over the last 25 years.

13.2 From "Health for All" to "Health as Investment"

In September 2011, the United Nations General Assembly convened a high-level meeting to address the prevention and control of non-communicable diseases (NCDs). It was only the second time in history that such a meeting had been devoted

[1] My analysis builds on theoretical work in sociology and in science and technology studies concerned with processes of economization (Berman 2013; Çalışkan and Callon 2009; Fourcade 2009; Mitchell 2006; Murphy 2013b). Michelle Murphy's work on the "economization of life" is particularly relevant here (Murphy 2013a).

to a topic related to health, the first having been in response to the HIV/AIDs pandemic a decade earlier. Unlike the earlier meeting, at which the vast majority of the burden of HIV/AIDs was acknowledged to fall on the countries of Sub-Saharan Africa, the 2011 summit presented the threat posed by NCDs as universal (United Nations General Assembly 2001). Far from the diseases of affluence that cancers, diabetes, and hypertension were once portrayed to be, NCDs had by late 2011 come to occupy a central place on the global health agenda. The precise *kind* of threat that NCDs were seen to present was not limited to the domain of health: the UN Resolution adopted by the General Assembly declared that "the global burden and threat of non-communicable diseases constitutes one of the major challenges for development in the twenty-first century" and that "non-communicable diseases are a threat to the economies of many Member States" (United Nations General Assembly 2012). A report by the World Health Organization (WHO) and the World Economic Forum (WEF) published to coincide with the UN NCD summit similarly warned that "The economic consequences of NCDs are staggering" with projected losses to low and middle income countries surpassing 4% of their annual output ("From Burden to 'Best Buys:' Reducing the Economic Impact of Non-Communicable Diseases in Low- and Middle-Income Countries" 2011, 3). Another report projected that the cost of NCDs to the global economy would exceed US$30 trillion over the next 20 years (Bloom et al. 2011, 5). By contrast, the cost of implementing a range of "best buy" interventions to prevent NCDs was low. The report continued: "[...] the return on this investment will be many millions of avoided premature deaths [...and] many billions of dollars of additional output" (2011, 3). NCDs are here positioned by the UN, by the WHO and by the WEF as a threat to both the health of the population and as a threat to the economy. Conversely, strategies to combat NCDs are imaged as a solid investment in health and in economic growth with an expected yield of positive future returns.

Just twenty-five earlier, in 1978, the World Health Organization celebrated the thirtieth anniversary of its founding with a conference on primary health care at Alma-Ata in the Soviet Union. There, the famous Alma-Ata declaration was made in which the WHO reaffirmed that "health, which is a state of complete physical, mental and social wellbeing, and not merely the absence of disease or infirmity, is a fundamental human right." "[T]he attainment of the highest possible level of health," the declaration continued, "is a most important world-wide social goal whose realization requires the action of many other social and economic sectors in addition to the health sector" ("Declaration of Alma-Ata" 1978). Famously, the WHO committed itself to the goal of achieving "health for all by the year 2000." In contrast to the UN NCD Declaration in 2013, this earlier declaration positioned health as both a human right and as a "most important world-wide social goal" – one that the resources of the economic sector must be harnessed to support.

How did the conceptualization of health that underpins world health efforts transition from an end-in-itself to a means towards economic growth? What prompted the transition from "health for all" to "health as investment?" Put differently, what explains the *economization* of global health over the past 25 years?

13.3 World Health and the World Bank

Throughout the 1980s the field of international health was beset by a number of tensions: debate over comprehensive vs selective primary health care, vertical vs horizontal approaches to health interventions, and budgetary crisis as well as crises of legitimacy at the World Health Organization. Although the conference at Alma-Ata represented a high point in the history of the WHO, it also marked the beginning of a long, slow decline in the organization's prominence. After Alma-Ata, the goal of "health for all" came to be seen by influential parties such as the United States Government, UNICEF and the Rockerfeller Foundation as overly ambitious and unrealistic (Birn et al. 2009; Brown et al. 2006; Cueto 2004). Without disavowing the *goal* of health for all, they began to advocate a different means by which to accomplish it. As opposed to what was now termed "Comprehensive Primary Health Care" (CPHP), these actors articulated a vision of "Selective Primary Health Care" (SPHC) emphasizing specific, low cost technical interventions that were limited in scope and easy to monitor and evaluate (Balabanova et al. 2013; Walsh and Warren 1979). Specifically, SPHC advocated a four-pronged approach to reducing child mortality known by the acronym GOBI: Growth monitoring (to ensure early detecting of childhood malnutrition), Oral Rehydration Solutions (for diarrheal diseases), Breastfeeding (for improved infant survival and natural family planning) and Immunization against certain communicable diseases. While successful in improving child survival the SPHC approach drew criticism from advocates of a broader-based *comprehensive* primary health care approach. The growing tension between advocates of SPHC and CPHC caused considerable tension at the WHO.

Against this backdrop, the World Bank "moved confidently into the vacuum created by an increasingly ineffective WHO" (Brown et al. 2006, 86). Although the Bank's initial interest in health extended only to population control, by the early 1980s the newly founded Population, Health and Nutrition Department began lending for stand-alone alone health programs on the rationale that enhanced health and nutrition would lead to increased economic growth (World Bank 1980). However, with World Bank money came their associated structural adjustment policies, which, in the domain of health focused on more efficient use of available resources and an increased role for the private sector in financing health services – all in service of promoting health for economic growth. While this approach drew much criticism from those who opposed privatization of the health sector, it did not stem the influence of the Bank and by 1990 World Bank lending for health surpassed the entire WHO budget (Brown et al. 2006). From the late 1980s to the late 1990s, Bank lending for health, nutrition and population projects grew sevenfold – with a growing proportion of these loans made with the explicit intention of reforming the structure of health systems (Fair 2008).[2]

The changing structural organization of international health coincided with a shift in the field's conceptualization of its primary targets due to "health transition." A pre-transitional environment dominated by high fertility and high mortality was seen to be giving way to a low mortality, low fertility environment (Frenk et al. 1989). While the

[2] During the late 1970s, fewer than 10% of World Bank Population, Health and Nutrition loans included "systemic" objectives. By the late 1990s, this number had risen to well over 50% (Fair 2008, 10).

health transition held general implications for the orientation of the world health agenda – away from population control and towards diseases of old-age, for example – the precise consequences of the transition for the global incidence of disease and for the exact interventions necessary to curb its spread were unknown. This knowledge deficit presented a two-fold problem for the Bank. First, while the Bank was interested in helping to reform health systems to provide a package of "essential health services" it was unclear to which diseases these services should be targeted. Second, in the absence of systematic estimates of the global burden of disease, statistics on disease prevalence were frequently provided by disease-specific advocates. These numbers were viewed with deep suspicion by World Bank health experts (Jamison et al. 1993; Murray and Lopez 1996; World Bank 1993). The Bank thus undertook a wide-reaching Health Sector Priorities Review which yielded a constellation of studies – most significantly the Disease Control Priorities Project (DCPP) (Jamison et al. 1993) and the Global Burden of Disease Study (GBD) (Murray and Lopez 1996). Results from both of these projects served as background to the landmark *World Development Report 1993: Investing in Health* (World Bank 1993), the publication of which is frequently cited as a watershed moment in the transition from international to global health. Importantly for my purposes, the *World Development Report 1993* (WDR 1993) also introduced the Disability Adjusted Life Year metric.

13.4 The DALY Metric

The architects of the DALY metric devised their new method for measuring the global burden of disease in order to account for the "full loss of healthy life" due to disease, death and disability on a global scale and to determine global health priorities according to cost-benefit analyses (Lopez 2005). Previous attempts to gauge the relative importance of different diseases used mortality statistics, disease prevalence rates, or risk of death calculations to determine the *number* of deaths due to various diseases (Feachem et al. 1992). The DALY metric, in contrast, sought to account also for the *burden* of diseases and conditions that may not be fatal, but by virtue of their duration and disabling effects contributed to economic "losses" in the form of diminished productivity and strain on health systems.[3] The DALY metric thus used "life-years" as a smaller and more commensurable unit than calculations made in terms of individual human lives.[4]

In its simplest presentation the DALY metric expresses "years of life lost to premature death and years lived with a disability of specified severity and duration" (Murray and Lopez 1996b, 7).

$$\text{DALYs} = YLL + YLD$$

[3] Ayo Wahlberg and Nikolas Rose have analyzed the DALY metric and disease *burden* concept as part of a longer history of what they call the "governmentalization of living" (Wahlberg and Rose 2015).

[4] While not the focus of the present paper, it is important to note also that by disaggregating lives into "life years", the DALY metric also provided a unit-measure with which to perform cost effectiveness analyses without appearing to put a dollar value on individual human lives.

However, a more technical description can be found in the WDR 1993, which explains that the DALY metric "measures the present value of the future stream of disability-free life lost as a result of death, disease, or injury" (World Bank 1993, 27). This measurement is made using a number of econometric techniques. I focus on two: age weighting and discounting.[5]

13.4.1 Age Weighting

Age weighting gives different value to years of life lost at different stages of the life course. It was incorporated into the DALY metric by "consensus judgment" in order to reflect the idea that "most societies attach more importance to a year of life lived by a young or middle-aged adult than to a year of life lived by a child or an elderly person" (World Bank 1993, 26 & 213). However, even if life was held to have the same *intrinsic* value at every age, one might still "attach greater importance to years of productive adult life" because of the importance of adults as "net producers" i.e. for their increased human capital and resulting contribution to economic growth (Murray and Lopez 1996). As a result of age weighting, the relative value of life rises steeply from zero at birth to its peak at age 25 before falling gradually with advancing age. The precise values used for DALY calculations were chosen so that the total number of DALYs is the same as though uniform age weights had been used (World Bank 1993, 213). But age weighting redistributes DALYs away from the early and later years and concentrate them on the middle, economically productive years of life – i.e. those years most critical to the Bank's priority of economic growth.

13.4.2 Discounting

The DALY metric also incorporates a discount rate (of 3%) such that future years of healthy life are valued at progressively lower levels into the future. This reflects what the GBD authors saw as a general societal preference for immediate gains: "[…] societies typically prefer to have a given amount of consumption today rather than tomorrow" (World Bank 1993, 213). However, the inclusion of this purportedly "typical" social value also has considerable consequences for the distribution of DALYs. Like age weighting, discounting results in the relatively greater valuing of economically productive middle years of life because the future years of life lost from

[5]Other components of the DALY metric include the severity weights that are used for calculating the impact of disability and the use of a global standardized life expectancy. Disability weights have been debated extensively in the scientific literature (Anand and Hanson 1997; Anand et al. 2004). I discuss both of these additional components of the DALY metric in my forthcoming dissertation. For my purposes here, it is important simply to note that economic productivity is also central to the determination of disability weights in so far as the ability to perform in one's occupation is a key feature of the disability weighting scale.

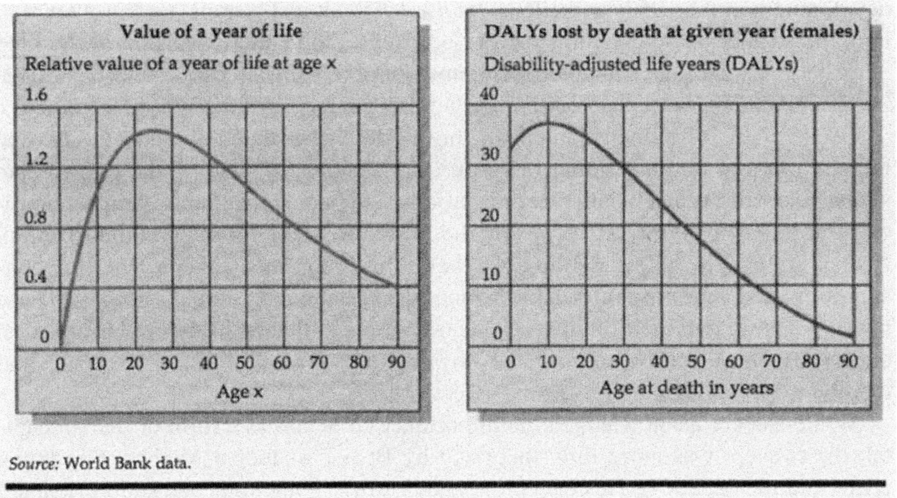

Fig. 13.1 Age weighting and resulting DALYs lost from early death (Reproduced from World Bank 1993, 26)

childhood deaths is discounted over a longer period. The contribution of childhood deaths to the global burden of disease is thus given relatively less *numerical* significance. As the GBD authors acknowledge "[...] higher discount rates reduce the importance of premature deaths at young ages in relation to those at older ages" (WDR 214).

The incorporation of age weighting and discounting functions into the DALY metric minimizes the contribution of childhood deaths to the global burden of disease and puts relatively greater value on the middle economically productive years of life – precisely those years deemed most important by the Bank for increasing economic growth. Figure 13.1 illustrates the age weighting function and the combined impact of age weighting and discounting on the resulting DALYs lost to death at different ages across the life course.

The relatively greater weighting of the middle, economically productive years of life in DALY calculations reflects a central tenet of the field of health economics as it has developed since the 1970s and 1980s: the conceptualization of health as a form of human capital.

13.4.3 Health as Human Capital

Each of the technical dimensions of the DALY metrics is underpinned by a general conceptualization of health as a form of "human capital"– a Nobel-prize winning approach within the field of economics developed by the Chicago School's Theodore Schultz and Gary Becker (Becker 1962; Schultz 1961). Although human capital theory met with resistance and controversy upon its initial introduction and development in the 1950s and 1960s, by the 1990s, it had become a central tenet of both micro and macro economic theory and key to the rapid expansion of the field of economics through so-called economic imperialism (Becker 1992; Fourcade 2006; Fourcade-Gourinchas 2001; Mitchell 2006).

Becker defined human capital as those "activities that influence future real income through the imbedding of resources in people" including the knowledge, skills, dispositions and health that are embodied in people that make them economically productive (1962, 9). Some of the ways to invest in one's human capital, Becker argued "include schooling, on-the-job training, medical care, vitamin consumption, and acquiring information about the economic system" (1962, 9). These investments vary in their relative effects on earnings, that is, in their relative return on investment. "But all improve the physical and mental abilities of people and thereby raise real income prospects" (Becker 1962, 9).

While Becker acknowledged the importance of health as a form of human capital, the concept was more fully theorized by Becker's student Michael Grossman (Grossman 1972, 2004). He conceptualized health as something consumers demand for two reasons. First, as a consumption commodity it "enters into their preference functions," that is, people prefer a state of health over a state of ill health. Second, and importantly for the argument here, health is conceptualized as an investment commodity because it "determines the total amount of time available for market and nonmarket activities [… such that] an increase in the stock of health reduces the time lost from these activities [i.e. time away from market and non-market activities]" (Grossman 1972, 225). Investing in one's health extends the *duration* of possible participation in market and non-market activity and maximizes the term over which investment in one's human capital can be realized.

The DALY metric was designed for the purposes of carrying out cost-benefit analyses of potential health interventions so as to design economically rational health systems. But more than just facilitating cost-benefit analyses, the DALY metric accomplishes an *economization of health* by imagining health as a form of human capital.

13.5 NDCs on the Global Health Agenda

Because of the higher valuing of economically productive middle years of life in DALY calculations, disease of middle age – notably NCDs – achieved greater prominence in the Global Burden of Disease (GBD) results (Murray and Lopez 1996, World Bank 1993). Before the introduction of the DALY metric, the then-current most comprehensive study of adult health worldwide concluded that "mortality from non-communicable diseases declines as overall mortality declines" (Feachem et al. 1992, 94). This suggested that as countries' death rates declined as they entered "health transition" so too would NCDs. However, after the introduction of the DALY metric just a few years later, the GBD would report that NCDs represented the single largest category of DALYs lost worldwide – greater than either communicable diseases or injuries (Murray and Lopez 1996). Furthermore, it would predict that by 2020 NCDs would account for more than 70% of deaths in developing regions (Murray and Lopez 1996). At the same time, the Disease Control Priorities Project (DCPP), also sponsored by the World Bank, would make a strong case for cost effectiveness of health interventions designed to mitigate NCD risks – notably those directed towards personal behavior change (Jamison et al. 1993).

The introduction of the DALY metric by the World Bank's World Development Report 1993: *Investing in health* brought NCDs into clear focus on the global health agenda. And this focus was further institutionalized in the early 2000s when the WHO officially adopted the DALY metric for purposes of disease quantification and cost-effectiveness analyses for purposes of priority setting (World Health Organization 2000). By September 2011, NCDs had come to occupy such a central position on the global health agenda as to warrant a UN High Level Summit meeting – only the second such meeting in the history of the UN.

13.6 Conclusion

The creation of the DALY metric by the World Bank in the early 1990s brought NCDs firmly onto the global health agenda. However, as this paper has suggested, the DALY logic by which NCDs became a global health priority depends on a vision of health as a form of human capital and as a site of investment. This can be seen in some of the more technical dimensions of the DALY metric, age weighting and discounting, for example. The political implications of the DALY metric – the redistribution of DALYs away from childhood disease and diseases of old age and towards the middle, economically productive years of life – are frequently obscured by the apparent objectivity of the numbers produced by DALY calculations. Yet these implications remain inseparable from the rising prominence of the World Bank in world health affairs since the late 1980s, its efforts to restructure health systems according to cost effectiveness, and its greater valuing of the economically productive middle years of life so as to prioritize health for economic growth.

More generally, the creation of the DALY metric and concomitant rise of NCDs as a global health priority coincides with the broader shift from international health to global health that has occurred over the last 25 years. The causes and consequences of this shift have only recently begun to receive sustained scholarly attention (Anderson 2014; Lakoff 2010; McGoey et al. 2011; Wahlberg and Rose 2015). But in this paper, I have suggested that this transition may productively be understood in relationship to the rise of economic rationalities in the field of world health. In contrast to a post-war vision of health as a human right and social good – a vision that came to be enshrined in the Alta Ata declaration of 1978 – the contemporary era of global health conceptualizes health as a form of human capital and as a site of investment. The transition from "health for all" to "health as investment," then, can be understood in relation to the economization of world health at the dawn of the twenty first century.

Acknowledgements This article draws on dissertation research that received financial support from the National Science Foundation (Grant #1059102) and the University of California Institute on Global Conflict and Cooperation.

Bibliography

Anand, S., and K. Hanson. 1997. Disability-Adjusted Life Years: A Critical Review. *Journal of Health Economics* 16(6): 685–702.

Anand, S., F. Peter, and A. Sen (eds.). 2004. *Public Health, Ethics, and Equity*. Oxford: Oxford University Press.

Anderson, W. 2014. Making Global Health History: The Postcolonial Worldliness of Biomedicine. *Social History of Medicine* 272: 372–384.

Balabanova, D., A. Mills, L. Conteh, B. Akkazieva, H. Banteyerga, U. Dash, and M. McKee. 2013. Good Health at Low Cost 25 years on: Lessons for the Future of Health Systems Strengthening. *Lancet* 381: 2118–2133.

Banta, J.E. 2001. From International Health to Global Health. *Journal of Community Health* 262: 73–76.

Becker, G. 1962. Investment in Human Capital: A Theoretical Analysis. *The Journal of Political Economy* 70(5): 9–49.

Becker, G.S. 1992. The Economic Way of Looking at Life. *Nobel Lectures, Economics*: 1991–1995.

Berman, E.P. 2013. Not Just Neoliberalism: Economization in US Science and Technology Policy. *Science, Technology & Human Values* 393: 397–431.

Birn, A.-E., Y. Pillay, and T.H. Holtz. 2009. *Textbook of International Health: Global Health in a Dynamic World*. 3rd ed. Oxford: Oxford University Press.

Bloom, D.E., E.T. Cafiero, E. Jané-Llopis, S. Abrahams-Gessel, L.R. Bloom, S. Fathima, A.B. Feigl, T. Gaziano, M. Mowafi, A. Pandya, K. Prettner, L. Rosenberg, B. Seligman, A.Z. Stein, and C. Weinstein. 2011. *The Global Economic Burden of Non-communicable Diseases*. Geneva: World Economic Forum.

Brown, T.M., M. Cueto, and E. Fee. 2006. The World Health Organization and the Transition from "International" to "Global" Public Health. *American Journal of Public Health* 961: 62–72.

Çalışkan, K., and M. Callon. 2009. Economization, Part 1: Shifting Attention from the Economy Towards Processes of Economization. *Economy and Society* 383: 369–398.

Chorev, N. 2012. *The World Health Organization between North and South*. Ithaca: Cornell University Press.

Cueto, M. 2004. The Origins of Primary Health Care and Selective Primary Health Care. *American Journal of Public Health* 9411: 1864–1874.

Declaration of Alma-Ata. 1978. International Conference on Primary Health Care, Alma-Ata, USSR.

Fair, M. 2008. *From Population Lending to HNP Results : The Evolution of the World Bank's Strategies in Health , Nutrition and Population*. Washington, DC: The World Bank.

Feachem, R.G.A., T. Kjellstrom, C.J.L. Murray, M. Over, and M.A. Phillips. 1992. *The Health of Adults in the Developing World*. New York/London: Oxford University Press on behalf of the World Bank.

Fourcade, M. 2006. The Construction of a Global Profession: The Transnationalization of Economics. *American Journal of Sociology* 1121: 145–194.

———. 2009. The Political Valuation of Life. *Regulation & Governance* 3: 291–297.

Fourcade-Gourinchas, M. 2001. Politics, Institutional Structures, and the Rise of Economics: A Comparative Study. *Theory & Society* 30: 397–447.

Frenk, J., J. Bobadilla, J. Sepulveda, and M.L. Cervantes. 1989. Health Transition in Middle-Income Countries: New Challenges for Health Care. *Health Policy and Planning* 4: 29–39.

Fried, L.P., M.E. Bentley, P. Buekens, D.S. Burke, J.J. Frenk, M.J. Klag, and H.C. Spencer. 2010. Global Health is Public Health. *Lancet* 375: 535–537.

From Burden to "Best Buys": Reducing the Economic Impact of Non-Communicable Diseases in Low- and Middle-Income Countries - prepared by the World Economic Forum and the Harvard School of Public Health. 2011. Available through: http://www.weforum.org/EconomicsOfNCD

Grossman, M. 1972. On the Concept of Health Capital and the Demand for Health. *Journal of Political Economy* 802: 223–255.

———. 2004. The Demand for Health, 30 Years Later: A Very Personal Retrospective and Prospective Reflection. *Journal of Health Economics* 234: 629–636.

Jamison, D.T., W.H. Mosely, A.R. Measham, and J.L. Bobadilla, eds. 1993. *Disease Control Priorities in Developing Countries*. New York: Oxford University Press on behalf of the World Bank.

Kenny, K. 2015. The Biopolitics of Global Health: Life and Death in Neoliberal Time. *Journal of Sociology* 51(1): 9–27.

Kleinman, A. 2010. Four Social Theories for Global Health. *The Lancet* 3759: 1518–1519.

Koplan, J.P., T.C. Bond, M.H. Merson, K.S. Reddy, M.H. Rodriguez, N.K. Sewankambo, and J.N. Wasserheit. 2009. Towards a Common Definition of Global Health. *Lancet* 3739: 1993–1995.

Lakoff, A. 2010. Two Regimes of Global Health. *Humanity: An International Journal of Human Rights, Humanitarianism, and Development* 1: 59–79.

Lakoff, A., and S.J. Collier. 2008. *Biosecurity Interventions: Global Health and Security in Question*. New York: Columbia University Press.

Lopez, A.D. 2005. The Evolution of the Global Burden of Disease Framework for Disease, Injury and Risk Factor Quantification: Developing the Evidence Base for National, Regional and Global Public Health Action. *Globalization and Health* 1: 5.

McCarthy, M. 2002. What's Going on at the World Health Organization? *Lancet* 3609: 1108–1110.

McCoy, D., S. Chand, and D. Sridhar. 2009. Global Health Funding: How Much, Where it Comes from and Where it Goes. *Health Policy and Planning* 246: 407–417.

McGoey, L., J. Reiss, and A. Wahlberg. 2011. The Global Health Complex. *BioSocieties* 6: 1–9.

Mitchell, T. 2006. The Work of Economics: How a Discipline Makes its World. *European Journal of Sociology* 46: 297–320.

Murphy, M. 2013a. Economization of Life: Calculative Infrastructures of Population and Economy. In *Relational Ecologies: Subjectivity, Sex, Nature and Architecture*, ed. P. Rawes. London: Routledge.

———. 2013b. The Girl: Mergers of Feminism and Finance in Neoliberal Times. *The Scholar & Feminist Online*, 11.1–11.2 Spring, 531–4.

Murray, C.J.L., and A.D. Lopez, eds. 1996. *The Global Burden of Disease: A Comprehensive Assessment of Mortality and Disability from Diseases, Injuries and Risk Gactors in 1990 and Projected to 2020*. Boston: Harvard School of Public Health on Behalf of the World Health Organization and the World Bank.

Ruger, J.P. 2005. The Changing Role of the World Bank in Global Health. *American Journal of Public Health* 95: 60–70.

Schultz, T. 1961. Investment in Human Capital. *The American Economic Review* 51(1): 1–17.

Thomas, C., and M. Weber. 2004. Whatever Happened to "Health for All by the Year 2000"? *Global Health Governance* 10: 187–205.

United Nations General Assembly. 2001. Resolution adopted by the General Assembly, *A/RES/S-26*.

———. 2012. Resolution adopted by the General Assembly.

Wahlberg, A., and N. Rose. 2015. Global Health and the Governmentalization of Living. *Economy and Society* 44: 60–90.

Walsh, J.A., and K.S. Warren. 1979. Selective Primary Health Care: An Interim Strategy for Disease Control in Developing Countries. *The New England Journal of Medicine* 301: 967–974.

World Bank. 1980. *World Development Report 1980*. Washington, DC: The World Bank.

———. 1993. *World Development Report 1993: Investing in Health*. Oxford: Oxford University Press.

World Health Organization. 2000. *World Health Report 2000: Health Systems: Improving Performance*. Geneva, Switzerland.

Chapter 14
The Economic Rationality of "Doing Good to Do Well" and Three Critiques, 1990 to the Present

Christian Olaf Christiansen

14.1 The Rise of Civic Capitalism – Doing Well by Doing Good

In the aftermath of economic globalisation, which accelerated after the collapse of the Eastern Bloc, a number of critiques of the increasingly globalised capitalism were articulated. These consisted, among other things, in a renewed environmental critique, in a critique of a series of violations against human rights by corporations, and, more generally, poor wage and working conditions in many countries of the so-called "third world" (or global south), in a critique of unfair trade agreements, and in a critique of ethically unsound corporate practices, as it was seen in spectacular corporate scandals as Enron in 2001 or in the exposure of scandalous working conditions in some of the textile industries world-known brands such as Tommy Hilfiger or Nike.

In the aftermath of these critiques of existing capitalist practices there has arisen a tremendous interest in corporate social responsibility (Smith 2003, 53; Vogel 2005a, b, 71–72). Today it has become a widespread ideal to unite profitability with "social value" into a higher synthesis. As Colin Crouch (2006, 1534) notes in his definition of CSR, it "is essentially 'corporate externality recognition'". Today, pure self-centeredness is often morally delegitimized in favour of contributing to the common good. Corporations articulate values, codes of conduct, and visions for the development of the company and its role in society, that highlights not just the economic, but also the social value corporations have for society. Another key concept is that of "corporate citizenship," emphasizing the role of the corporation as a "citizen" in society (Carroll 1991, 43). New networks and movements have arisen that confronts "economism." An illustrative example is the international network

C.O. Christiansen (✉)
Institute for Culture and Society, Aarhus University, Aarhus, Denmark
e-mail: idecoc@cas.au.dk

J. Bek-Thomsen et al. (eds.), *History of Economic Rationalities*, Ethical Economy 54, DOI 10.1007/978-3-319-52815-1_14

Humanism in Business, whose vision it is to contribute to a fundamental change (transformation) of economic rationality, so that economic activities, especially corporations', becomes human and "life"-serving, instead of solely serving profit-making and economic growth (Spitzeck et al. 2009). The enthusiasm for a new, enlightened and socially responsible capitalism can also be found among left wing think tanks as well as economic historians (Callahan 2008; Jacoby 1997). Even business schools change their curricula and are increasingly preoccupied with CSR and business ethics. A whole industry has evolved with consultants and PR-people who are working with social branding of companies, and influential academic institutions such as the American management organization, *Academy of Management*, has in recent years announced key annual conference themes such as *Doing Well by Doing Good* (2007) and *Green Management Matters* (2009). The economically liberal *The Economist* has acknowledged that capitalism finds itself in a new crisis of legitimacy, spawned by the ongoing financial crises, and that there is much need for new thinking in relation to e.g. concepts such as CSR (Economist 2011, 70). And the perhaps most prominent contributor to business strategy, Michael Porter, has distanced himself from short-sighted shareholder-capitalism, suggesting instead to focus upon "shared value," taking consideration of the environment, sustainability, and labour and consumer markets in developing countries (Porter and Kramer 2011). Similarly, there has been introduced new "bottom lines" such as social, ethical and green accountancy techniques. Some advocate a new, enlightened self-interest, whose basic idea is that it is in the own best interest of companies to think in longer terms, and to improve the "ethical quality" of company practices (Smith 2003). There is also a significant interest in what is typically referred to as social entrepreneurship, which often also tries to combine financial goals with "extra" social value, i.e. when market forces are used strategically with the stated intend of reaching social goals (Paine 2009; Yunus 2009). CSR has become a norm (Vogel 2010, 79; Gond et al. 2011, 653). Many observers agree that an important way in which capitalism is today being justified is through the idea of social responsibility and of corporations' positive role in society, and the merging of profitability with "extra" social value (Banerjee 2007; Kazmi et al. 2008; Reich 2007; Shamir 2004a, b; Vogel 2005b).

What we have seen rise during the 1990s and 2000s is "civic capitalism." Corporations are increasingly spoken of as responsible citizens in a society in which there are many stakeholders. Companies are expected to be virtuous citizens, citizens who not only have an economic responsibility for their self-preservation, but also a moral responsibility in relation to the many economic, social and environmental circuits they are a part of. The role of the citizen traditionally involves a concern for the common good, and the concept of civic capitalism captures this increased responsibilization of companies.

Civic capitalism can be seen as capitalism's contemporary response to the social and environmental critiques which were raised against it during the 1990s and 2000s. In prolongation of Boltanski and Chiapello, civic capitalism can fruitfully be theorised as a new "spirit" of capitalism. First, it links together the overall transformation of society with a motivational level through new justifications and legitimisations of a capitalism which is both creating profits *and* doing good at the same time – adding economic value as well as social value. The spirit of a civic capitalism provides new *meaning*: we are not just in it for the profits, but also to add social value. Second, the concept of "spirit" is appropriate here because "civic capitalism" can partly be seen as a response to critique (to "naming and shaming" campaigns by activists, to public scepticism about corporations, etc.), and the concept of "civic capitalism" thus draws upon Boltanski and Chiapello's (2002, 2007) account of the dynamical relationship between the spirit of capitalism and the critique of capitalism (Christiansen 2010, 25–29).

14.2 Why Civic Capitalism?

There are several plausible reasons that can help explain the big enthusiasm for "civic capitalism." To unite profitability with "social" value is to combine two highly acclaimed goals, and it is often claimed that there are no conflicts between these goals. Not least has the so-called "business case for virtue" very often been advocated. If a better ethical behaviour actually pays off in dollars and cents, this will give companies the incentive to act more ethically (That there seems to be scant evidence for "the business case for virtue" is another part of the story, cf. Vogel 2005a, 2010, 82). Furthermore, civic capitalism places corporations in a positive new light, contributes to their legitimacy, public image, and employee motivation (Dierksmeier 2009). It may attract "young idealists" as well as it can seem attractive to the generation which witnessed the legitimacy crisis of capitalism in the 1960s and 1970s, and who have possibly been longing for another way of describing the purpose of doing business (Vogel 2005b). It contributes to enthusiasm for academics who are involved in management and organizational research, and who can now see their own research in connection with the new reconciliation of social and financial goals (Kazmi et al. 2009, 673). Also, the political and public system seems to be relieved when corporations take responsibility for public tasks (Reich 2007, 170). Finally, new markets for the provision of welfare goods are opened when the state and the public sector withdraw.

Civic capitalism is nourished by scepticism of an identity of interests between corporations and society. It does not seem too surprising that the ideal of harmonising financial goals (profits) with social goals has become popular as a guideline for practice. If profitability and social goals can be united in a higher synthesis, what critical concerns have to be raised against this brave new world of a civic capitalism, which will benefit everybody?

14.3 Critiquing Civic Capitalism (1): On the Gap Between Rhetoric and Practice

One form of critique of civic capitalism consists in constantly testing relationships between discourse and practice of corporations. Scholars have pointed towards many "progressive effects" and potentials connected to civic capitalism. For example, David Vogel notes that more and more corporations have signed up for the UN global compact initiative originally launched in 2001 (Vogel 2005a, b, cf. e.g. pp. 71–72), and that there has been many achievements since CSR started spreading in the 1990s, such as reduction of the use of child labour, reduction of carbon emissions, etc. by "leading" CSR firms (ibid., especially 162–163). On the other hand, research shows that there often (but not always) is a significant gap between the rhetoric of corporations and their actual conduct (as, for example, in the cases of BP and Enron) (Banerjee 2007, 2008). This argument has perhaps most influentially been advocated by organizational researcher Subhabrata Banerjee, who has detailed how CSR and stakeholder theory, despite the win-win rhetoric, has often been used with the sole purpose of promoting business interests, and has been used actively by corporations to keep government and regulation at bay.

Yet, the "soft" corporate rhetoric is not *only* and *not always* "just" rhetoric. It is along these lines that legal sociologist Ronen Shamir refers to a *moralization of the market* (2008a). According to Shamir, a whole *field* around CSR has arisen, with a host of different actors. On the one hand, new demands for CSR are being raised by the public, by consumers, by interest organizations, civil rights movements, local stakeholders, etc. On the other hand, corporations and business organizations have often tried actively to conquer the CSR-discourse – to define and to interpret what CSR is and how it should be managed (Shamir 2004a, b). Shamir documents that CSR has partly been a strategic site of intervention for corporations, sometimes in order to avoid "hard law" instead of the "soft law" of e.g. corporations' subscriptions to codes of conduct.

The point to be stressed here is that CSR from this perspective is also a concept which has been used *against* corporations. Looking at this complex field as a whole, it does not make sense completely to reduce CSR to nothing but a clever marketing instrument invented by corporations, or to being an "ideology of the ruling class." It is rather a *battle concept*: there is a battle concerned with interpreting it, defining it, and applying it. The concept is used to legitimize, as well as to *delegitimize*, the conduct of corporations (and the global capitalist market system as such). Legitimacy may have an economic cost when not all types of economic processes and accumulation of profits are seen as legitimate. In terms of the sociology of critique, corporations thereby "expose" themselves to different kinds of tests. These can be more or less institutionalized – ranging from communicated, loose commitments other actors can act upon, to industry codes, code-of-conduct statements, international certification systems, to CSR-reporting to nation states, etc. If a corporation is committed to the rhetoric of civic capitalism, it runs the risk that someone actually holds it responsible for its commitments. In this sense, the economic rationality of a "civic capitalism" which is legitimised by dedifferentiating a pure logic business and a social rationale, opens up for a particular kind of critique, namely the testing of the relationship between discourse and practice.

14.4 Critiquing Civic Capitalism (2): Ethical Shortcomings

Another type of critique, often taken up in the field of academic business ethics, investigates civic capitalism from an ethical point of view: how can one ethically (from the point of view of moral philosophy) assess the "quality" of different dimensions of civic capitalism such as CSR, social entrepreneurship, corporate philanthropy etc.? One main critique of civic capitalism here is that social and moral questions are often *transformed* when they are being dealt with from a business rationality (Shamir 2008a; Ulrich 2008). Critics suggest that social and moral questions lose their independent status when they are considered from the point of view of being business opportunities and business risks – of whether morally unsound activities may be "worth the risk," or when e.g. philanthropy is undertaken solely as an economic investment in a brand.

Economic philosophy and business ethics have tried to clarify that the kind of ethics which is typically assumed here is a utilitarian ethics, which balances positive and negative economic consequences against one another. For example, the Swiss business ethicist and economic philosopher Peter Ulrich has from a Kantian perspective and a so-called "republican liberalism" argued that the most widespread forms of business ethics rank economic utility (profits) above what Ulrich calls "basic moral duties" (Ulrich 2008, 389ff). Ulrich outlines a continuum which shows a trade-off between the profit principle and a deontological, Kantian principle, which says that every human being should always be treated also as an end in itself, not just as a means. In one end of this spectrum Ulrich finds what he refers to as the "instrumentalist business ethic," that which demands that "ethic pays;" this is exclusively focused upon consequences, and according to Ulrich, it thus violates the intrinsic value of basic moral duties, because it subordinates them to the profit principle. Next to this "instrumentalist business ethic" Ulrich positions an ethic of charity or the *post festum* ethics. This can be illustrated with the metaphor of a cake: First it is made, and then it is distributed. According to Ulrich, this business ethic (philanthropy) does not constitute a radical anti-thesis to the principle of profit maximization; rather, philanthropy embodies an *utilitarian fiction* in which it is assumed that the subsequent redistribution can somehow outweigh whatever negative consequences there were part of initially "baking" the cake. A second type of criticism of civic capitalism has thus been identified: the ethical critique or "test" of civic capitalism which seeks to clarify the conditions, assumptions, etc. by which practices of civic capitalism can be seen as ethical or not, and in which respect.

14.5 Critiquing Civic Capitalism (3): Democratic Shortcomings

A third type of criticism deals with civic capitalism from a democratic or governance perspective, looking at the role civic capitalism plays in the complex relationships between businesses, state, civil society etc. One claim is that civic capitalism may actually work to hinder *democratic ways* for curbing capitalism, as e.g. through a certain measure of universal welfare rights and a democratic and legal containment of capitalism (cf. also Vogel 2005a, 2010). When corporations are constructed as responsible, moral agents, there seems to be less need for political regulation and legislation which would put capitalism under democratic control. Critics thus argue that there is a trade-off between civic capitalism and of democratic politics as two different modes of governance. Instead of legislation which sets up boundaries for which activities are legal, based upon a democratic process, civic capitalism offers itself as an alternative road which in the name of "enlightened capitalism" says "no" to political and legal regulation. As Robert Reich (2007) has observed, politicians can then resort to a moral critique of singular business enterprises, as well as moral appraisal of others, whereas political solutions to common challenges are given up upon.

Along similar lines, Ronen Shamir has argued that in the aftermath of the so-called ACTA-law suits in the United States against multinational corporations who typically were accused of violating human rights in non-Western countries, what typically happened was that corporations pleaded themselves non-guilty of the different accusations, and then actively tried to promote their engagement in CSR (Shamir 2004a, b). They recommended so-called 'soft law' initiatives, first and foremost based upon the principle of voluntariness and self-regulation, instead of top down political and legal regulation.

The idea of civic capitalism gives the impression that capitalism in itself is not only democratic, but also plastic, efficient, and de-central, which makes it possible that problems are solved where they occur, instead of new regulation imposed by a distant and centralized bureaucratic state. In prolongation of Thomas Frank (2000) it can be argued that civic capitalism is related to what he conceptualises as "market populism," understood as the idea that the market is essentially democratic (one dollar, one vote; allocations through the market mechanism are results of free actors choices, i.e. buying and selling on the market), and plastic enough to incorporate all kinds of societal problems. Even though civic capitalism critiques greedy and "excessive" self-interest, its insistence upon the principles of voluntariness and self-regulation are then actually a confirmation of the dogma that problems are best solved locally by parties directly involved, and by market fundamentalism (Shamir 2008b).

Furthermore, critics have argued that business leaders do not have any special authority as decision makers when it comes to major issues of society's interest (Reich 2007). The argument is then, again, that civic capitalism involves an undermining of the trust in democracy, as a new horizon of expectations gradually arises in which the expectations for private actors to act increases, whereas the expectations for democratic politics is diminished. Ronen Shamir has claimed that what can be seen is a structural coupling between, on the one hand, the moralisation of the market (responsibilisation of market actors), and the marketization of the public and of politics. Private actors are "responsibilised," and are thereby equipped to further taking care of traditional care and welfare tasks; public actors are also responsibilised, but in order to act on the premises of the market.

14.6 Conclusion

This chapter has explored the recent decades' rapid spreading of a discourse which says that business and profitability can be combined with ethical conduct and social concerns. I have argued that this idea of combining business with "doing good" can be theorised as a new "spirit" of capitalism. More specifically, I have suggested that it can be dubbed a spirit of "civic" capitalism, as corporations are discursively constructed as socially responsible (virtuous) citizens in society. This spirit of civic capitalism offers an economic rationale for doing good at the same time as it offers business a language of social legitimacy. Critics, however, draw upon at least three different types of critique of civic capitalism: a *reality check*, asking whether corporations actually practice what they preach (i.e. do the good they make promises to do); an *ethical check*, asking about which kinds of ethics is typically assumed in e.g. mainstream CSR or corporate philanthropy; and a *democratic check*, investigating the spread of e.g. CSR in the context of overall distribution of responsibilities between business, state, government and civil society.

Bibliography

Banerjee, S.B. 2007. *Corporate Social Responsibility: The Good, the Bad and the Ugly*. Cheltenham: Edward Elgar.

———. 2008. Corporate Social Responsibility: The Good, the Bad and the Ugly. *Critical Sociology* 34(1): 51–79.

Boltanski, L. and È. Chiapello 2002. *The New Spirit of Capitalism*, Paper presented at the conference of Europeanists, March 14–16, 2002, Chicago. http://www.sociologia.unimib.it/mastersqs/rivi/boltan.pdf. Visited 20 Aug 2004.

Boltanski, L., and È. Chiapello. 2007. *The New Spirit of Capitalism*. London: Verso.

Boltanski, L., and L. Thévenot. 2006. *On Justification: Economies of Worth*. Princeton: Princeton University Press.

Callahan, D. 2008. A Gentler Capitalism. A Sea Change May be Afoot in How American Business Views Its Role in Society. *LA Times*, January 31st, 2008.

Carroll, A.B. 1991. The Pyramid of Corporate Social Responsibility: Toward the Moral Management of Organizational Stakeholders. *Business Horizons* 34(1): 39–48.

Christiansen, C.O. 2010. Lost in Translation: Bringing Hirschman's Concept of Voice Back into the Spirit of Capitalism. *Management and Organizational History* 5(1): 19–35.

Crouch, C. 2006. Modelling the Firm in its Market and Organizational Environment: Methodologies for Studying Corporate Social Responsibility. *Organization Studies* 27(10): 1533–1551.
Dierksmeier, C. 2009. A Requisite Journey: From Business Ethics to Economic Philosophy. In *Humanism in Business*, ed. H. Spitzeck et al., 68–83. Cambridge, MA: Cambridge University Press.
Frank, T. 2000. *One Market Under God: Extreme Capitalism, Market Populism, and the End of Economic Democracy*. New York: Random House.
Gond, Jean-Pascal, Nahee Kang, and Jeremy Moon. 2011. The Government of Self-Regulation: On the Comparative Dynamics of Corporate Social Responsibility. *Economy and Society* 40(4): 640–671.
Jacoby, S.M. 1997. *Modern Manors: Welfare Capitalism Since the New Deal*. Princeton: Princeton University Press.
Kazmi, B.H., B. Leca, and P. Naccache 2008. *Corporate Social Responsibility: The Brand New Spirit of Capitalism?* Unpublished conference paper presented at the Academy of Management annual meeting 2008, Los Angeles, Critical Management Studies pre-conference workshop.
Kazmi, B.A., B. Leca, and P. Naccache. 2009. Book Review: Subhabrata Bobby Banerjee: Corporate Social Responsibility: The Good, the Bad and the Ugly. *Organization Studies* 30(6): 673–684.
Paine, L.S. 2009. The Value Shift: Merging Social and Financial Imperatives. In *Humanism in Business*, ed. H. Spitzeck et al., 204–217. Cambridge, MA: Cambridge University Press.
Porter, M.E., and M.R. Kramer. 2011. Creating Shared Value: How to Reinvent Capitalism – and Unleash a Wave of Innovation and Growth. *Harvard Business Review* 89(1/2): 62–77.
Reich, R.B. 2007. *Supercapitalism: The Transformation of Business, Democracy, and Everyday Life*. New York: Alfred A. Knopf.
Shamir, R. 2004a. The De-Radicalization of Corporate Social Responsibility. *Critical Sociology* 30(3): 669–689.
———. 2004b. Between Self-Regulation and the Alien Tort Claims Act: On the Contested Concept of Corporate Social Responsibility. *Law & Society Review* 38(4): 635–664.
———. 2005. Mind the Gap: The Commodification of Corporate Social Responsibility. *Symbolic Interaction* 28(2): 229–253.
———. 2008a. The Age of Responsibilization: On Market-Embedded Morality. *Economy and Society* 37(1): 1–19.
———. 2008b. Corporate Social Responsibility: Towards a New Market-Embedded Morality? *Theoretical Inquiries in Law* 9(2): 371–394.
Smith, N.C. 2003. Corporate Social Responsibility: Whether or How? *California Management Review* 45(4): 42–76.
Spitzeck, H., M. Pirson, W. Amann, S. Khan, and E.V. Kimakowitz. 2009. Introduction. In *Humanism in Business*, ed. H. Spitzeck et al., 1–12. Cambridge, MA: Cambridge University Press.
The Economist. 2011. *Schumpeters Blog: 'Oh, Mr Porter'*, March 12th, p. 70.
Ulrich, P. 2008. *Integrative Economic Ethics: Foundations of a Civilised Market Economy*. Cambridge, MA: Cambridge University Press.
Vogel, D. 2005a. *The Market for Virtue: The Potential and Limits of Corporate Social Responsibility*. Washington, D.C.: Brookings Institution Press.
———. 2005b. Is There a Market for Virtue? The Business Case for Corporate Social Responsibility. *California Management Review* 47(4): 19–45.
———. 2010. The Private Regulation of Global Corporate Conduct: Achievements and Limitations. *Business & Society* 49(1): 68–87.
Yunus, M. 2009. Social Business Entrepreneurs are the Solution. In *Humanism in Business*, ed. H. Spitzeck et al., 402–412. Cambridge, MA: Cambridge University Press.